D0131587

# iPad Pro
## Guide

The Ultimate Guide for
iPad Pro & iPadOS

# Introduction

## Welcome to **iPad Pro** Guide

iPads are everywhere. You'll find them in people's backpacks, next to their beds, sitting on coffee tables.... you get the idea. What I'm getting at, is that a lot of people know how to use the iPad. Most children know how to use an iPad. Maybe it's because with a touchscreen, you can just reach out and touch whatever you want to interact with.

Of course, there's much more to iPad Pro than just a touchscreen. It's possibly the most advanced piece of technology created by man, with components designed at the nanometer scale, and with software that can learn your routine, habits, and interests. That's what this book is all about. It's about revealing the features and abilities of the iPad, but in a *human* way. You won't find any technical mumbo-jumbo, nor will it ramble on about features that most users don't need to know about. Instead, it will reveal the basics of the iPad, like what it's hardware does, how it's built-in apps work, and how you can use an iPad to enrich and improve your life. It will also include some short, snippy, humorous tips now and then, just to liven things up.

Just before I go, if there's anything you would like to know that isn't covered in this book, send me an email at tom@leafpublishing.co.uk, and I'll be more than happy to help.

**Tom Rudderham, Author**

### About the author

Tom Rudderham is the author of iPad Pro Guide, iPhone XS Guide, MacBook Pro Guide, Photos: the Ultimate Guide to iPhone & iPad Photography, iPad: Interactive Guide, and much more.

Tom kicked off his writing career at Future Publishing, working for magazines including MacFormat, Computer Arts, Imagine FX, and the Official Windows Magazine. Later, he became a User Experience and Interface Designer, researching, planning, and designing websites and apps for companies including Siemens, Waitrose, the IOPC, Amigo Loans, and Microsoft.

Since 2012, he has written a large range of best-selling technology books and manuals, covering every major Apple product since the launch of the iPhone 5.

**Published by:**
Leaf Publishing LTD
www.leafpublishing.co.uk

**ISBN:**
9781549854774

**Copyright © 2020 by Leaf Publishing LTD**

All rights reserved. No part of this publication may be reproduced, stored or transmitted in any form or by any means, electronic, mechanical, photocopying, recording, scanning, or otherwise without written permission from the publisher. It is illegal to copy this book, post it to a website, or distribute it by any other means without permission.

# Contents

## Welcome

## Accessories

## Apps

## The Basics

# Welcome

The iPad Pro is the most advanced tablet device available, with an operating system that's years ahead of the competition. But unlike every computer you've ever used before, the iPad is a delight to interact with. It's simple, elegant and packed with possibilities...

# Terminology

## Wondering what all those words and phrases mean?

The iPad is a state of the art piece of equipment, so perhaps it's inevitable that talking about it involves using a wide-ranging assortment of words, phrases, and terminology. In this book, you're going to hear a lot about the iPad hardware, software, and features. Don't worry, each one of them will be explained as we go, so you'll never feel confused or get lost halfway through a paragraph. To get you started, here are a few of the words we will be using constantly throughout this book...

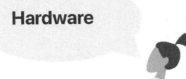

**Hardware**

Whenever the word hardware is used, we're basically talking about the iPad in its physical form. The thing which you hold in your hand.

**Software**

Think of software as a set of instructions for doing something on your iPad. These instructions might be millions of words long, and they were probably written by a large team of people. To most humans, it's utter gibberish. It looks something like this:

```
int main(int argc, char * argv[]) {
    @autoreleasepool {
        return UIApplicationMain( argc, argv, nil,
NSStringFromClass( [AVCamAppDelegate
class] ) );
    }
```

To a programmer who writes in Swift (Apple's programming language), this makes perfect sense. It's just a fraction of the code required to tell your iPad how to capture an image using its camera. The full piece of code is tens of thousands of lines long.

**App**

The word app is short for application. An application is a piece of software, separate from iOS, which lets you do something. There's an app on your iPad for taking a picture. There's an app for sending messages. There's an app for looking at your photos. I'm sure you get the idea.

## iOS

This is the name of the software which powers your iPad. It's one of the most complicated pieces of software ever created by man. It tells your iPad how to turn on, how to take a photo, how to browse the internet, how to scan your face when you want to unlock your iPad, plus so much more. It can also learn over time. iOS will learn about your habits, how you type to individual people, where you travel, what you look like and what you sound like. It uses all of this learning to help you type quicker, find photos quicker, and basically use your iPad in a more efficient manner.

You don't have to worry about security either, because all of this personal information is fully encrypted, and the really important stuff, like your voice and face information, never leaves your iPad.

When most people think of the word iOS, they imagine the home screen of their iPad. The place where all the icons are which let you open the internet browser or email application. You can think of it like that too, but really, it's so much more.

## Third-party apps

These are apps created by companies other than Apple. There are literately millions of them, and each app serves its own purpose. The most common apps you'll find include Facebook, Instagram, Amazon, and Netflix, but you can also find apps which let you add silly graphics onto photos, access your bank account, play games, and more. You'll find all of these apps in the...

## App Store

Think of the App Store as a market for apps. Some apps are free, others cost a few dollars/pounds/euros. Some apps look like they are free, but ask for a payment to do something (this is called an "In-App Purchase"). You can find the App Store on your iPad. It has a bright blue icon with an abstract "A" in the middle.

## Encryption

Think of encryption as a padlock for words, but instead of 0-9 on the padlock, it's A-Z, plus 0-9. The software on your iPad uses encryption all the time. Whenever you send a message to a friend, all the letters you type are scrambled up, sent to the other person, then de-scrambled on their device. The same goes for video calls you make using FaceTime, your credit cards details when you check out on the internet, and much more. Nearly everything you do on your iPad is encrypted, which is why even the FBI can't access your phone without your password or biometric information.

## iCloud

Think of iCloud as a computer somewhere in the world where your photos, messages, apps, and settings are stored. Your iPad talks to this computer over the internet everyday to backup new photos, send new messages, and check for updates.

# A brief history of the iPad

## A look at how far we've come...

It was the morning of January 27, 2010, that the late Steve Jobs walked onto stage to unveil the iPad. It was a day long-expected by the world's media. For month's prior there had been rumors that the company behind the Mac and iPhone was working on a tablet computer that would change the world. Leaked images had appeared on the web showing a partially covered prototype displaying Google Maps. Shortly afterward, Steve was overheard saying *"This will be the most important thing I've ever done."* There was a fervent buzz in the air.

## 2010
# iPad

As Steve unveiled the iPad for the very first time, he told the audience: *"The iPad is really thin. It's half an inch thin, and it weighs just one and a half pounds. That is thinner and lighter than ANY netbook."*

Alongside its impressive dimensions, the original iPad featured a 9.7-inch LED display with a resolution of just 1024x768 pixels. It was powered by a custom-designed A4 chip, along with 256MB of RAM. It didn't include a camera and was charged by a traditional 30-pin Dock connector.

Its operating system was based on the iPhone OS (at the time version 3.2). It included most of the same apps but with updated interfaces designed to take advantage of the larger display. Launched alongside the iPad were several brand new apps, including Pages, Numbers, and Keynote, enabling users to edit and create documents, spreadsheets and presentations.

The Wi-Fi-only version of iPad went on sale April 3rd, 2010, selling more than 300,000 units in its first weekend alone. One month later, when the iPad with Wi-Fi+3G launched, it had sold a combined one million units, making the iPad the first commercially successful tablet computer.

## 2011
# iPad 2

As Game of Thrones fans recovered from the shock of the first season's finale, the iPad 2 was unleashed upon the world.

The iPad 2 was lighter at 1.33 pounds, 33% thinner, and included both front and back cameras, enabling people to make FaceTime calls for the first time. It also included a gyroscope, making its basic features equal to the iPhone, with the exception of voice calling.

## 2012
# iPad 3rd gen.

It was the year that Barack Obama was inaugurated as the 44th President of the United States. It was also the year that the iPad gained a Retina Display, with a total pixel count of 2056x1536 - making it the highest-resolution tablet available. The 3rd generation iPad also included 4G compatibility, making wireless data transfer even faster than before.

## 2012
# iPad Mini

Debuting just a few months after the 3rd generation iPad, the iPad Mini came with a 7.9-inch non-Retina display. It was powered by the same processor as the iPad 2, but supported 4G compatibility and included both front and rear facing cameras.

To date, both the iPad 2 and the iPad Mini are the bestselling iPad models.

## 2012
# iPad 4th gen.

2012 was a busy year for the iPad. It saw the 3rd generation iPad release, on March 16th, followed by both the iPad Mini and the 4th generation iPad on November 2nd.

There was a good reason for the sudden release of the 4th generation iPad, because it introduced the Apple A6X processor, which massively improved responsiveness and overall speed. The 4th gen iPad also included a Lightning port for the first time.

## 2013
# iPad Mini 2

This was the year that twerking became a thing, while China landed a rover vehicle on the Moon. It was also the year that Apple launched the iPad Mini 2.

The Mini 2 included a 2,048×1,536 resolution Retina Display, making text and imagery incredibly crisp on its 7.9-inch display. It also included the A7 chip, shared by its larger sibling, the...

## 2013
# iPad Air

With a thinner design than its predecessor, a powerful 64-bit processor, and the all-new iOS 7 operating system, the iPad proved to be a massive hit with consumers.

The UK Editor of TechRadar, Patrick Gloss, said *"It's hard to put into words how much Apple has improved the iPad, offering a stunning level of detail and power with a build quality that's unrivaled."*

## 2014
# iPad Mini 3

It seemed like the long-promised gaming revolution known as virtual reality was about to be realized in 2014, when the Oculus Rift developer kit unit became available to buy. It ushered in a new, immersive world of gaming that brought worlds to life like never before, but it was also buggy and plagued by a low-resolution screen.

The iPad Mini 3 wasn't the most radical of updates. Internally it was identical to its predecessor, but externally it came in a fetching new gold color. It also introduced Touch ID to the iPad lineup, enabling users to unlock their iPad or make a purchase online using just their fingertip.

## 2014
# iPad Air 2

The iPad Air 2 was a beast for its time. It introduced a triple-core A8X processor, an 8-core GPU, and doubled the internal memory from 1GB to 2GB. Like the iPad Mini 3, it also came in a gold color and included a Touch ID sensor for fingerprint recognition.

## 2015
# iPad Mini 4

The iPad Mini 4 is essentially an iPad Air 2 shrunk down to fit inside a smaller case. It has the same specifications as the Air 2, but with two exceptions: a smaller Retina Display, and a dual-core A8 processor, instead of the tri-core A8X.

## 2015
# 12.9-inch iPad Pro

Since its release in 2011, the iPad has become the main computing device for millions of people.

Thanks to its simple user interface and large Multi-Touch display, it has enabled them to browse the web, enjoy a TV show and communicate with friends and family in a simple but immersive way. There has never been a more intuitive device for those new to the world of computing and the world wide web. That was until September 9th, 2015, when the iPad Pro was announced at Apple's 'Hey Siri' event.

With an even larger 12.9-inch display, increased performance and support for both Apple Pencil and the Smart Keyboard, the iPad Pro promised to enable millions more to create and engage with content in entirely new ways. For the first time, it was possible to draw and write on the iPad display, use two full-sized apps simultaneously, or write an essay using the Smart Keyboard.

With 5.6 million pixels, the 12.9-inch display on the iPad Pro was 78% larger than the iPad Air 2 display; in fact, the width of the iPad Pro display was the same as the height of an iPad Air display, which meant two full-size apps could be run side-by-side in landscape mode, without compromising on functionality.

Other improvements to iPad Pro included four high-fidelity speakers in each corner of the unit. This produced a more engaging sound, with three times the acoustic output of the iPad Air. A new Smart Connector also prevented dust and water from entering the device, while also removing the need to physically plug and connect a keyboard.

## 2016
# iPad Pro 9.7-inch

Announced March 21st, 2016, the iPad Pro 9.7-inch was the answer to those who found the 12.9-inch model just a little bit too big. On the outside, it didn't look much different from the iPad Air 2, with the exception of 4 speaker grills and a smart connector for the keyboard. It even weighed the same as the iPad Air 2 and featured the same dimensions. Internally, however, there was a vast new set of features and specifications that really set the Pro model part.

The 9.7-inch iPad Pro featured the A9X chip and Apple M9 Motion coprocessor, although it's worth noting that the 9.7-inch model was slightly under-clocked at 2.16 GHz, compared to 2.26 GHz on the 12.9-inch model. It had a better camera, bumped from 8MP to 12MP, and was the first iPad to include both True Tone Flash and Retina Flash. It also had a True Tone display, which enabled the LCD to adapt to ambient lighting to change its color and intensity to match the environment.

## 2017
# iPad Pro 10.5-inch

What could be better than a 9.7-inch iPad Pro? How about an iPad that's similar in size, but features a bigger screen? That's exactly what was introduced to the world at WWDC on June 5th 2017, alongside a 12.9-inch iPad Pro with updated specifications.

Both models of iPad Pro now supported up to 512GB of storage, both came with an A10X six-core CPU, and both included a 12-core GPU; making them the most powerful mobile devices ever shipped from Apple.

The screen was perhaps the most impressive new feature announced for the 10.5-inch iPad Pro. It was 20% larger than the 9.7-inch model, was brighter than before, and was coated with the same anti-reflective coating found on iMacs and MacBook Pros. It also included a new technology called "ProMotion". In short, ProMotion could refresh the pixels of the screen up to 120x a second, making scrolling and zooming smoother than ever before. To save battery life the screen could also update at a lower 24x a second when viewing still images and content.

## 2018
# iPad Pro

The 2018 iPad Pro marked the most significant change to the iPad to since its introduction in 2011. In many ways, it was the iPad people dreamed about when they imagined what a tablet should be.

For the year prior to the new iPad Pro announcement, Apple managed to eliminate large bezels from half of its product line. It started with the iPhone X, continued with the Apple Watch, and then finally, the iPad Pro recieved the same treatment: an edge-to-edge LCD that enveloped nearly the entire device.

Apple achieved this design by rounding the corners of the display, using the same pixel masking and anti-aliasing technology which was introduced with the iPhone XR. Apple called this technology the Liquid Retina display. Packed beneath its glass were a number of technologies, such as P3 wide color support, Pro-Motion, and support for Apple Pencil.

Eliminating the bezels was just the first step in upgrading the 2018 iPad Pro, because beneath its display was a massive amount of new technology, such as a Face ID sensor, a desktop-class A12 X processor, and better speakers.

Two new sizes of iPad were also introduced. The first maintained the same size and footprint as the original 10.5-inch iPad Pro, but the screen was now larger, at 11-inches. Half an inch might not sound like much, but it delivered a vastly improved experience when browsing the web or creating rich media. It also meant that a quarter of a million extra pixels were packed within the display.

For customers who wanted an even larger canvas, the 12.9-inch iPad still remained, but in a vastly smaller package. With smaller bezels and no Home button, the 12.9-inch iPad Pro was almost exactly the same size as an 8.5 x 11-inch piece of paper.

## 2020
# iPad Pro

An entirely new camera system, faster internals, and double the storage make the 2020 iPad a powerful alternative to traditional desktop computing.

Glance at either the 11-inch and 12.9-inch iPad and you might struggle to tell them apart from the 2018 models. That's because from the front and the sides, they look identical in every way. It's not until you look around the back that you'll notice a pretty big difference: a dual camera system with a LIDAR scanner for depth sensing and AR.

This all-new camera system is a massive upgrade over previous iPads. The 12MP camera and the 10MP ultra-wide camera are both borrowed from the iPhone 11. They take amazing photos - even in low light conditions. The LIDAR scanner is the first of its kind on any type of computing device. With support from third-party apps, it should enable faster and more accurace AR experiences, such as games which blend with the real world around you. With time, it might also enable you to take more accurate Portrait Mode photos.

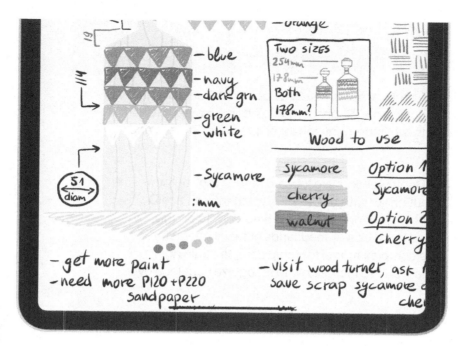

## Liquid Retina Display

The Liquid Retina display which dominates the front of iPad Pro is a beautiful thing to behold. Perhaps that's because of the sheer size of the display, which makes it possible to create content or enjoy media in a way that isn't possible on the iPhone.

The Liquid Retina display on the iPad Pro 11-inch has a resolution of 2388x1668 at 264 pixels per inch. The 12.9-inch model has a resolution of 2732x2048, also at 264 pixels per inch. That's the same density as the previous iPad Pros, so if you've upgraded from any of those devices, then you'll be familiar with how sharp it looks.

Both displays support the P3 wide color range, for richer reds, and more vibrant greens, but at 600 nits maximum brightness support, they're not quite bright enough to support the full HDR format. Apple defines the displays on the iPad Pros as "EDR" compatible, which stands for extended dynamic range. This means you can still download and watch HDR-supported content, like the latest shows from Netflix, and they will look nearly HDR in color and brightness quality; but the only way to truly watch them in HDR is to use a USB-C cable, then mirror your iPad's display on a HDR-supported screen.

An anti-reflective coating has been applied to the iPad Pro display, to help hide reflections and glare across the screen, and it's better than any previous iPad, or any of Apple's other portable devices. It can also hold up over time to heavy-duty Apple Pencil use, and the tens of thousands of prods and pokes that come with being a multitouch display.

One obvious difference between the latest iPhones and the iPad Pro is a lack of a notch. Because of its relative size, the bezels around the iPad Pro are just large enough to house some of the most sophisticated technology ever developed for an iPad. Called the TrueDepth Camera System, it contains the following sensors and emitters to enable face recognition:

* Ambient light sensor
* Speaker
* Proximity Sensor
* Flood Illuminator
* Microphone
* 7MP camera
* Infrared Camera
* Dot Projector

The TrueDepth Camera System enables you to unlock your iPad using just your face. Introduced alongside the iPhone X in 2017, it has proved to be a more efficient system than the fingerprint sensor on previous iPhones and iPads.

On the iPad Pro, the TrueDepth sensors are located at the "top" of the device in portrait mode, but unlike with the iPhone, you can use FaceID to unlock your device in whichever orientation the iPad is in. To do this, the team at Apple captured hundreds of thousands of facial geometry samples, to create a more complex model for more complex training; which basically means the iPad Pro learns how to recognize your face over time.

Placing the TrueDepth camera on the top of the iPad Pro poses one small problem: if you're holding the iPad in landscape orientation, then the TrueDepth sensor can become blocked by your hand. The iPad will notify you if this happens, with a message on-screen that reads "Camera covered". It will also show an animated arrow pointing to where the camera is. With time, it becomes a natural habit to hold the iPad Pro in a way that doesn't cover the camera.

## Industrial Design

The iPad Pro features a design language that in many ways, is a throwback to the iPhone 4 from a decade earlier. Gone are the rounded edges and chamfered detailing found on the traditional iPad; instead, replaced with flat edges that fall off, and stark antenna lines that are hard to miss. It's industrial to behold, and surprisingly attractive in person. It moves the design language forward, while staying true to its heritage.

Some design choices from earlier iPad models remain, however. The power button is still at the top of the device, unlike on the side, as seen with the latest iPhone models, and the volume buttons remain on the upper-right side.

Beneath the volume buttons, centered along the side of the iPad, is a magnetic connector for the Apple Pencil. Look around the back and you'll see the Smart Connector near the bottom of the iPad, which lets you wirelessly connect the new Magic Keyboard. Thanks to its clever design, the Smart Connector is both dust and waterproof, while also providing power to the keyboard.

By now you might have noticed that the traditional 3.5mm headphone socket no longer exists. Apple has been dropping support for 3.5mm headphones from its products for quite some time, which has helped them to introduce the bezel-to-bezel curved display (a 3.5mm socket goes deep into the device and prevents the LCD from reaching the edges). If you've already gone wireless with your headphones, then these will work perfectly with the iPad Pro; otherwise, you'll need to purchase a USB-C to 3.5mm Headphone Jack Adaptor from the Apple Store.

## A12Z Bionic

The iPad Pro has always been a competitor to notebooks when it comes to raw speed. The 2020 iPad Pro takes things further. It's faster than most laptops on the market today, and even faster than the 13-inch MacBook Pro, no matter which processor the notebook is configured with.

In short, the A12Z chip inside the iPad Pro is a *beast*. Its 7-nanometer design is based on the A12X Bionic from the previous iPad Pro; and it still retains a similar 8-core design. When compared to previous iPads, Apple says the A12Z chip is up to 35 percent faster on single-core performance, and up to 90 percent faster on multi-core processes.

The GPU (graphics processing unit) within the iPad Pro also features a 7-core design, which Apple says is comparable to an Xbox One in terms of graphics rendering. We're unlikely to see any games which can prove that in the near future, but for now, it's great for high-end professionals who demand the fastest GPUs for rendering imagery.

## Tech Specs

**Internals:**
11-inch screen: 2388x1668 LED
12.9-inch screen: 2732x2048 LED
Processor: A12Z Bionic chip
RAM: 6GB
Speakers: 4-speaker audio
Cameras: 12MP wide lens, 10MP ultra-wide lens, LIDAR scanner, and 7MP front-facing lens
11-inch Battery: 29.37-watt-hour
12.9-inch Battery: 36.71-watt-hour
Storage: 128GB / 256GB / 512GB / 1TB

**11-inch iPad Pro Dimensions:**
Height: 9.74"
Width: 7.02"
Thickness: 5.9mm
Weight: 468 grams

**12.9-inch iPad Pro Dimensions:**
Height: 11.04"
Width: 8.46"
Thickness: 5.9mm
Weight: 631 grams

# Cameras

Hold an iPad Pro in your hand, and the first thing you might *feel* is the camera bump around the back.

That's because the iPad Pro is thinner than the camera module mounted within, meaning the lenses now poke out of the back. On the downside, it means the iPad wobbles slightly when laid flat, but on the upside, the 2020 iPad Pro includes the same amazing lenses found on the iPhone 11.

The top camera is a new 12MP wide camera with a new sensor that has a faster autofocus. In low-light conditions, it's now up to 3X faster than the previous generation of the iPad. The lower lens is a brand new ultra-wide camera with a 120-degree field of view, enabling you to capture more in your photos, like a stunning landscape or a group shot. Think of it as an optical 2X zoom out, so you can capture more without moving.

The front-facing camera now supports limited 3D depth, to enable Portrait selfies and Memojis. This means you can now take selfie photos with a blurred background, to simulate traditional DSLR cameras, or bring your face to life with animated characters including a dinosaur, alien, or unicorn.

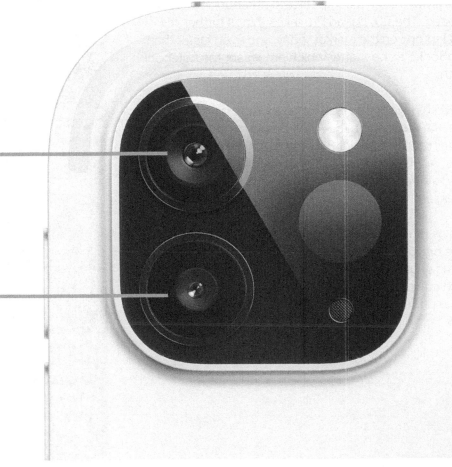

**Wide Camera**
- 26 mm focal length
- ƒ/1.8 aperture
- 6-element lens
- Optical image stabilization
- 100% Focus Pixels
- New 12MP sensor

**Ultra Wide Camera**
- 13 mm focal length
- f/2.4 aperture
- 5-element lens
- 120° field of view
- 4x more scene
- 10MP sensor

## LIDAR

By now you've probably noticed the mysterious grey circle on the camera bump. It's a custom-designed LiDAR scanner that uses direct time of flight to measure reflected light from up to five metres away, both indoors and out. In short, it can instantly work out the dimensions of the environment around to you to enable accurate 3D augmented reality experiences. This means you can place a virtual object in the room in front of you, then see objects pass both behind and in front of it. With time you can expect to see more immersive and realistic games and AR apps.

## Audio

More people than ever before are using their iPad to watch TV shows, movies, and stream video content, so it's essential that the audio speaker system is capable of producing rich, deep sound that carries across a room. The iPad Pro achieves this by using four high-fidelity speakers, with one in each corner. This layout produces an engaging sound with three times the acoustic output of the iPad Air, making video content and apps sound better than ever before. Additionally, the iPad Pro automatically adjusts the orientation of high-frequencies depending on how you're holding the device, ensuring that the top two speakers are always dedicated to higher frequencies.

# Accessories

The iPad Pro is unique among Apple's touchscreen-based devices in that it is totally transformed by using accessories. The Apple Pencil enables you to draw, paint, and annotate using a device that feels and reacts like a pencil, while the Magic Keyboard turns the iPad Pro into a fully-fledged laptop replacement.

This chapter will briefly cover these accessories and explain how each benefits the iPad Pro in entirely new ways.

# Apple Pencil

There might be times when your fingertip isn't accurate enough for a creative process. Perhaps you'd like to draw a beautiful illustration, but your fingertip is getting in the way; or maybe you'd like to accurately select and manipulate an object that's mere pixels in size. With Apple Pencil, you can do all of that, and more.

That's because the Apple Pencil is sensitive to both tilt and pressure, enabling you to create a range of artistic strokes and effects. You can press harder to create a thicker line, or tilt the Apple Pencil to create subtle curves and shading. Apple Pencil also feels natural to hold, and there's practically no lag between the movement of the Pencil tip and the on-screen response. Using Apple Pencil with the iPad Pro feels intimate, natural and intuitive. There are no buttons to learn, nor gestures to remember, just pick up Apple Pencil and start to draw.

### How does the Apple Pencil work?
To detect the pressure of input, the tip of Apple Pencil can move up and down in tandem with the force of your hand, and thanks to some incredibly intricate and accurate pressure sensors — as well as two tilt sensors – the Pencil can calculate the exact orientation and angle of your hand. Your iPad Pro recognizes when Apple Pencil is being used, so to prevent spurious inputs it turns off Multi-Touch recognition to stop your palm and fingers from sending signals to the display. Your iPad Pro also doubles its subsystem scan to 240 times per second, giving twice the data points for input. All this technology means you can quickly draw and sketch lines without the iPad missing a curve or swivel.

### It's tap sensitive
Whenever you want to change tools within an app, just double-tap the Apple Pencil. Using the Notes app, you can swap from the pen to the eraser with just two taps, and with third-party apps, you can configure the double-tap feature to suit your needs.

### It's magnetic too
The first generation of Apple Pencil was a bit fiddly to charge. First, you had to pull off its cap, then plug the top of the Pencil into the Lightning Port on the bottom of the iPad. The second generation of Apple Pencil supports wireless charging; so to charge it, just snap the Pencil to the side of your iPad and it will automatically start charging. The magnet is stronger than you might think too, so you can carry your iPad, or even shake it, and the Pencil won't drop off.

### Open the Notes app with a tap
If you want to quickly get into the Notes app on your iPad, then tap the screen with the tip of the Apple Pencil and you'll automatically unlock the device and jump straight into the Notes app.

### Supported Apps
So what apps support Apple Pencil out-of-the-box? There's Notes, which now enables you to draw, write and color with amazing accuracy; the Mail app now lets you annotate attachments, while third-party apps such as Paper let you sketch, write, draw and outline like a professional artist. More third-party apps can be expected in the near future as developers begin to take advantage of this amazing new tool.

# Smart Keyboard Folio

There's no denying that writing on the iPad Pro is a great experience. The display is large enough to accommodate a full-sized keyboard, while Multi-Touch capabilities let you access accent keys, emoji's and even turn the keyboard into a giant trackpad. So why would you want to buy the Smart Keyboard?

Well, for one it enables you to see a full-screen view of your document, art, or work. That's because as soon as you attach the Smart Keyboard, your iPad Pro automatically recognizes it, turns off the on-screen keyboard and lets you type with ease. Second, the Smart Keyboard acts as a robust cover for your iPad, protecting the screen when not in use while also acting as a stand for propping up the device during a movie. In short, this versatile, lightweight keyboard enables you to be more productive while also protecting the iPad Pro hardware.

So how does it work? A highly-durable fabric is laser-ablated to form the shape of each key. This provides a spring-like tension which mimics the feel of a traditional key while eliminating the need for traditional mechanisms. The fabric of the keyboard is water and stain-resistant, but only 4 millimeters thin to ensure the keyboard is slim and lightweight. Beneath the top layer is a conductive layer of fabric which reads each keystroke then seamlessly communicates each press back to the iPad Pro. It does this instantly, and without the need for wires, so you can enjoy a simple yet technologically advanced way to type.

**Take advantage of the shortcuts bar**
When the Smart Keyboard is attached to your iPad Pro, text-based apps such as Notes, Mail, and Pages automatically recognize the keyboard and offer a full-screen view of your work. However, look at the bottom of the screen and you'll see the shortcuts bar. You can use this to perform commands with the iPad, swap between apps, or bring up the search bar.

**Keyboard shortcuts**
While using a text-based app, hold down a key such as Command, Option, or Control, and you'll see which shortcuts work with the on-screen app. As an example, here are just a few of the shortcuts that work with Pages:

⌘ X = Cut
⌘ C = Copy
⌘ V = Paste
⌘ N = New Document
⌘ F = Search
⌘ D = Duplicate
⌘ shift W = Show Word Count
⌘ option C = Copy Style
⌘ option C = Paste Style

# Magic Keyboard

The all-new Magic Keyboard is an amazing companion for your iPad Pro. It features the best typing experience ever on iPad, with a scissor mechanism keyboard, a trackpad that opens up new ways to work with iPadOS, a USB-C port for pass-through charging, and front and back protection. The Magic Keyboard also features a floating cantilever design, allowing you to attach iPad Pro magnetically and smoothly adjust it to the perfect viewing angle for you.

**Compatible with:**
- iPad Pro 12.9-inch (3rd and 4th generation)
- iPad Pro 11-inch (1st and 2nd generation)

## Comfortable typing

Full-size, backlit keys ensure it's easy to type on the Magic Keyboard, even in the dark. The Magic Keyboard also features the same scissor mechanism found on the MacBook keyboard with 1 mm of travel, so typing is responsive yet quiet.

## Floating cantilever design

The iPad appears to float over the Magic Keyboard, suspended in the air by the a cantilever mecahnism. The angle of the iPad can also be adjusted to ensure the perfect viewing angle is available.

## Built-in trackpad

It's now possible to interact with your iPad Pro using gestures and a pointer, making it possible to easily select and manipulate text, spreadsheet cells, and more.

## Front and back protection

The Magic Keyboard also acts as a protective case for both the front and the back of the iPad Pro.

# How to use a trackpad or mouse

Use a pointer to select objects, manipulate text, and more...

The iPad Pro has always been a versatile device for day-to-day tasks such as browsing the web and creating basic documents, but with a trackpad or mouse, it's pretty much a replacement for the traditional computer. That's because a trackpad or mouse makes it possible to easily select text, move objects, and even manipulate spreadsheet cells. Best of all, iPadOS supports a number of gestures which enable you to fully control every part of the iPad experience, using just the trackpad or mouse. To get started, it's recommended that you use one of these three accessories:

| | | |
|---|---|---|
| **Magic Keyboard** | **Magic Trackpad 2** | **Magic Mouse 2** |
| Priced $299 for the 11-inch keyboard, or $349 for the 12.9-inch keyboard, this is a full-sized keyboard with scissor mechanism keys and a large Multi-Touch trackpad. It also includes a USB-C port for passthrough charging and front and back protection. | Traditionally included with the iMac, this stand-alone trackpad can automatically connect to the iPad Pro using Bluetooth. | Another accessory traditionally available for the Mac. If you've used a desktop computer in the past, then this will be a very familiar accessory to use with your iPad. |

## How to connect a Magic Trackpad or Mouse with your iPad

To connect the Magic Trackpad or Mouse to the iPad, open the **Settings** app, tap **Bluetooth**, then select the accessory. If you don't see it, make sure to unpair it from your Mac first.

## The basics of using the pointer

With a trackpad or mouse connected to your iPad, you'll see a circular pointer on the screen. This is called the pointer, and it moves around the screen as you slide your finger across the trackpad or move the mouse.

- **The pointer only appears when you need it.** The pointer isn't persistent at all times, instead only appearing when you're touching the trackpad or moving the mouse.

- **It can change shape based on what it's pointing at.** The pointer changes shape to be the size of the button or app below it, and if you move it over text, it turns into a thin vertical line. You can disable this by going to **Settings** > **Accessibility** > **Pointer Control**, then toggling **Pointer Animations** off.

### Wake your iPad

You can wake up your iPad by using a trackpad or mouse. Just click it and you'll see your iPad wake up.

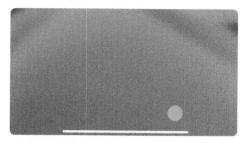

### Unlock your iPad

Move the pointer to the Home bar at the bottom of the screen and you'll automatically unlock your iPad.

### Right-click

You can right-click on apps, text, and objects to access the same secondary menu found when tapping and holding.

### Return to the Home Screen

To go home using the trackpad, swipe up with three fingers. If using a mouse, move the pointer to the Home bar then click on it.

### Access the Dock

To quickly access the Dock at anytime, move the pointer to the bottom of the screen.

### Access Control Center

To adjust settings or control music at any time, click the status icons in the upper-right corner to bring up Control Center.

### Access the multitasking screen

You can jump between apps or force-close them by swiping up and holding with three fingers.

### Jump between apps

You can swipe between open apps by swiping left and right with three fingers.

### Swipe between Slide Over apps

Move the pointer over the Slide Over app, then swipe using three fingers to jump between apps.

# The Basics

The iPad raises the bar for tablet technology, but it's just as intuitive and delightful to use as all previous iPads. This chapter will cover the very basics of using iPad. You'll discover its hardware, how to perform gestures, how to access Control Center, and much more.

# The iPad Pro hardware

## What all those holes, sensors, and buttons do...

The iPad Pro is a fairly simple device to use. There's a screen, some camera lenses around the back and a series of buttons around the edges. Here's what those buttons do:

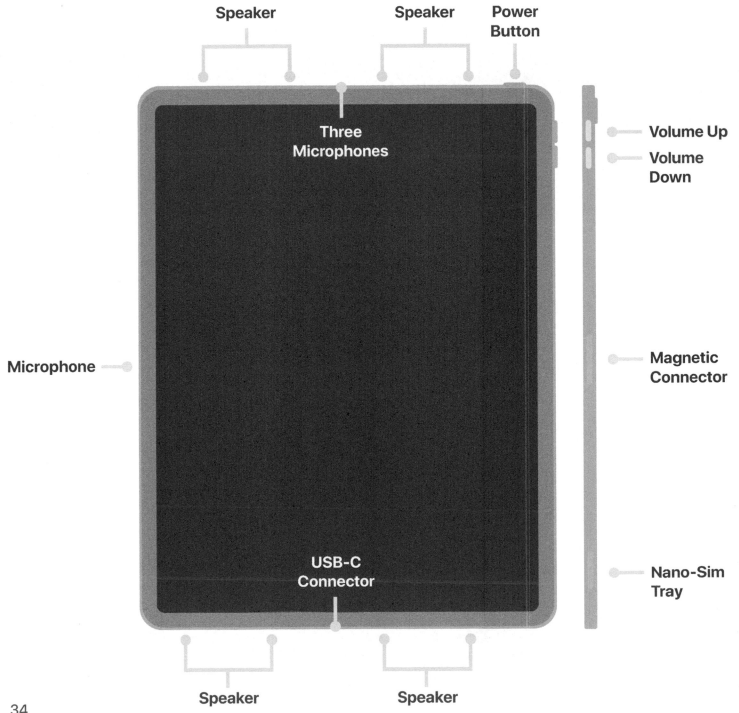

**Power Button**

**When off:**

- Press and hold to turn your iPad Pro on.

**When on:**

- Press it once to lock your iPad.
- Press and hold along with a volume button to turn off your iPad.
- Press and hold to enable Siri.
- Press it twice to access Apple Pay.

**Volume Up**

- Press once to turn the volume up.
- Press and hold to quickly turn the volume up.
- Press while using the Camera app to take a photo.
- Press simultaneously with the Power button to take a screenshot.

**Volume Down**

- Press once to turn the volume down.
- Press and hold to quickly mute the audio.
- Press while using the Camera app to take a photo.

# Setup and activate your iPad

Discover how to activate your brand new iPad Pro...

So you've bought a brand new iPad, and you've unwrapped it from the box. The next step is to activate it for the very first time. This process will let you choose a language to use, set your location and local time, and activate key features such as Siri (a helpful voice-activated assistant). Once your iPad is activated, you'll be able to use it to browse the web, send messages, plus much more.

## How to activate your iPad

1   Start by turning on your iPad for the first time. To do this, just press the **power** button on the top-right side. After a moment or two the Apple logo will appear.

2   When the Hello screen appears, **swipe up** from the bottom of the screen to continue.

3   Tap the language you want to use for your iPad, then tap the country or region.

## How to insert a SIM card

If you've purchased an iPad with a cellular connection, then the first thing you need to do is to insert a SIM card. This will let your iPad connect to the web if there's no Wi-Fi available.

1   Look in the iPad box for the SIM tray tool. It's thin, silver, and looks like a paperclip.

2   Insert the pointy end of the SIM tray tool into the small hole on the lower-right side of your iPad.

3   Press hard, and the sim tray will pop out slightly.

4   Use your fingernail to pull the sim tray out, then carefully place your SIM card into it. You might have to flip it around to make sure it fits property.

5   Slide the SIM tray back into your iPad and you're good to go.

*If you're moving from one iPad to another...*

## Use the Quick Start tool to copy across your old iPad

If you're going from an old iPad to a new one, then you can use the Quick Start tool to automatically copy across all of your messages, photos, apps, settings, and personal data to the new iPad. It works quickly and it's easy to do...

**1** Place your new iPad next to your old one. The Quick Start screen will automatically offer the option of using your Apple ID to set up the new device. Make sure it's the right Apple ID, then tap **Continue**.

**2** Wait for an animation to appear on your new iPad, then use the camera viewfinder on the old iPad and center the animation in the middle of the screen. When you see a button that says **Finish on New [Device]**, tap the button and follow the on-screen options to transfer your apps, data, and settings to the new device.

## Use the Quick Start tool to copy your data from iCloud

If you don't have your old iPad to hand, then you can sync all of your messages, apps, accounts, and other personal data from iCloud. To do this:

**1** After activating your iPad, tap **Restore from iCloud Backup**.

**2** Sign into iCloud using your Apple ID and password.

**3** Choose the most recent backup. You can check by looking at the date and size of each backup.

**4** If you've purchased apps and iTunes content using multiple Apple IDs, then you'll be asked for the passwords to each one.

**5** Wait for the process to finish. This may take some time, so it's a good idea to keep your device connected to Wi-Fi and a power source.

**6** After the process has completed your iPad will turn on and activate, but it will still need to download content such as apps and photos, so be patient as it restores all of your data.

# Face ID

## Learn how to setup Face ID so you can unlock your iPad using your face...

One of the most sci-fi features of the iPad Pro is its ability to instantly scan your face with a dot projector, then automatically unlock it or let you buy things. It's a feature called Face ID, and it's way more advanced than you might think.

It works by using a TrueDepth Camera System to recognize you. Basically, an infrared camera can see your face, even in the dark, while a dot projector maps your face with more than 30,000 dots. All of this data is used to create a mathematical model of your face. This mathematical model is used to prevent people from using photos of you to unlock your iPad. Face ID also looks for telltale signs of life (like moving or blinking eyes), to know that a model of your face wasn't used. Once it has confirmed all of this (which usually takes less than a second) then Face ID tells your iPad that it's definitely you; and that things are good to go.

Here's a neat little fact: when using Face ID, there's a 1 in a million chance that someone else can unlock your device by looking at it.

# How to set up Face ID

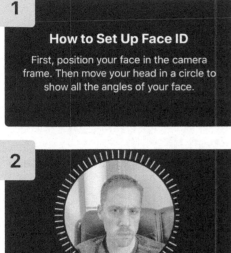

**1** Your iPad will ask you to setup Face ID when you activate it for the very first time. If you skipped that step, just open the **Settings** app, select **Face ID & Passcode** then tap **Enrol Face.**

**2** Follow the on-screen instructions to add your face. You'll be asked to gently move your head in a circular motion. That's because Face ID performs best when all angles of your face are captured.

**3** Once the process is complete, tap **Done** to enrol your face.

### Face ID is now set up.

### Set up an alternative look

If you sometimes change your look in a drastic way (for example via makeup, with a wig, or with extensive accessories), then you can teach Face ID to recognize you with these changes. To do this, get ready with your alternative look, then go to **Settings > Face ID & Passcode**, then tap **Set Up an Alternate Appearance**.

# The Lock Screen

## Use gestures to unlock your iPad, access Notification Center, and more...

Lift up your iPad and (so long as it's turned on) the Lock Screen will quickly fade into view. If you've received any notifications, such as a text message or a news story, then you'll see them in the middle of the screen. Otherwise, you'll just see the background wallpaper, time, and date.

If your iPad is on a desk and you don't want to pick it up, then you can also tap on the screen to display the Lock Screen.

Swipe down from the top-right corner to access Control Center.

Tap a notification to find out more, or swipe it to the left to manage any further notifications.

Swipe from the left to access Spotlight, where all your widgets, shortcuts and Spotlight search can be found.

Swipe up from the bottom of the screen to go to the Home Screen.

# The Home Screen

Discover how to interact with apps and folders...

From the Lock screen, swipe upwards from the bottom of the screen and your iPad will unlock and display the Home screen. You'll see multiple icons across the screen. These represent the apps installed on your iPad. To open one of these apps just tap on its icon. To close the app and go back to the Home screen, just swipe upwards from the bottom of the screen. You can also access the Dock at any time by swiping up from the bottom of the screen by just a small amount.

To make a folder of apps, tap and hold on an app icon, wait for the secondary menu to appear, then drag the app on top of another app.

- Tap and hold on an app icon to see a secondary menu.
- Tap and hold on an icon for 3 seconds or more to re-arrange or delete apps.

This is the Dock. You can put important apps here and you'll always find them at the bottom of the Home screen.

Apps you have recently opened will appear on the right-side of the Dock.

Swipe left or right across an empty part of the screen to see more apps.

# Gestures and buttons

Learn about key gestures used for controlling your iPad Pro...

The vast, high-definition screen that spreads out across your iPad is a technological marvel. You might not know it, but it actually supports up to 10 individual fingertips, and works by detecting the static charge on your skin — not heat or pressure as many often believe. By tapping and gesturing on the screen you can take full advantage of everything iOS has to offer, such as zooming into content, rotating images and more.

Additionally, the hardware buttons on your iPad enable you to activate Siri or shut the entire thing off. Many of these functions are entirely intuitive, but for those who have never interacted with an iPad before, let's go over them...

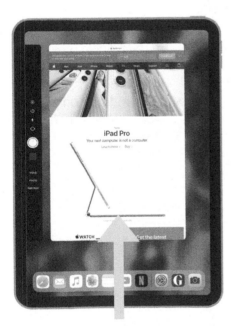  

### Return to the Home screen

Whenever you're in an app, swipe up quickly from the very bottom of the screen to return to the Home screen.

### Access the Dock

The Dock is where your favorite apps and most recently used apps are located. You'll see the Dock at the bottom of the Home screen, but you can also access it whenever you're in an app by swiping up from the bottom of the screen then stopping after an inch or two.

### Access the multitasking screen

Swipe up from the bottom of the screen then stop halfway to see all the apps you've recently opened. You can scroll through the app thumbnails, then tap on one to re-open it.

### Force quit an app

While you're viewing the multitasking screen, push an app thumbnail upwards and off the screen to force quit it. You only need to do this if an app has crashed and stopped working.

### Power off your device

If you'd like to fully turn off your iPad, then hold down both the **power** button and **volume up** buttons.

### Jump between apps

Want to quickly jump between apps? Swipe along the very bottom of the screen, left-to-right, and you'll jump between apps.

### Access Search

From the Home screen, pull the screen down using your finger to access the Search screen. From here you can search for apps, emails, contacts and more.

### Swipe to go back

To go back a panel or page, swipe from the left-side of the screen inwards. This works great in apps like Safari, Mail, or Settings.

### Access Siri

To talk to Siri press and hold the **Power** button on the top of your iPad. You can also say *"Hey Siri"* out-loud to enable Siri.

# How to use Control Center

Discover how to quickly toggle controls...

Tucked above the screen are a helpful set of shortcut buttons for toggling common switches and settings. They include a slider for controlling the screen brightness, a button for enabling Wi-Fi, shortcuts to toggle Airplane Mode, Night Shift mode, and more. To access these shortcuts at any time swipe down from the top-right corner of the screen. In an instant, you'll see Control Center appear as an overlay above the screen.

You can **tap and hold** on all of the buttons within Control Center to show further settings or controls. For example, by tapping and holding on the Music control panel you can access settings for scrubbing through the track, adjusting the volume, and enabling AirPlay.

To close Control Center swipe back up or tap in the empty space below Control Center.

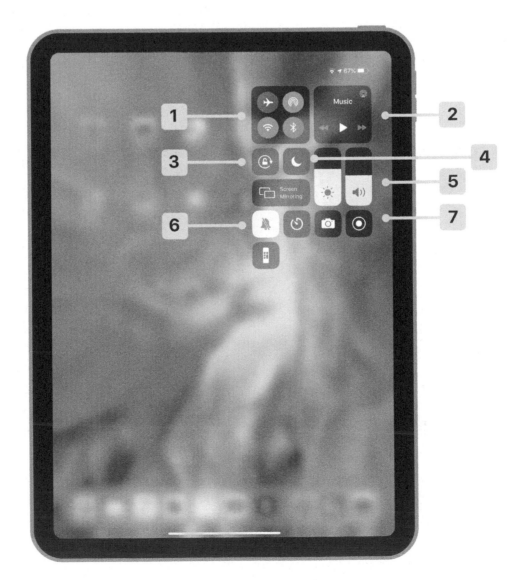

**1** **Network and connection settings**

The rounded box in the top-left corner of the screen is where you can access all the wireless and network settings for your iPad. By default, you'll see four controls for activating or disabling Airplane mode, your cellular connection, Wi-Fi, and Bluetooth.

**2** **Music controls**

The box in the upper-right portion of Control Center lets you control music playback and settings. By default you'll see the track name, play, and fast-forward/skip. If you have headphones connected, then in the top-right corner of the box will be a small icon (it looks like two curved lines) for choosing the playback device. By pressing and holding on this box you can expand it to show album artwork, a volume slider, and a timeline scrubber.

**3** **Orientation Lock**

If you don't want the screen to rotate into landscape/portrait mode when you rotate your iPad, then tap the **Orientation Lock** button.

**4** **Do Not Disturb**

Tap the **moon** icon to turn on Do Not Disturb. While it's on you won't be bothered by FaceTime calls, texts or any notifications, your iPad won't emit any noise and the screen won't turn on. Tap and hold on the moon icon, and you'll also be able to enable Do Not Disturb for a set period of time.

**5** **Brightness and volume sliders**

To the middle-right of Control Center are sliders for adjusting the display brightness and volume. Drag these sliders to make changes, or tap and hold on them to access larger controls which are easier to use.

**6** **Silent Mode**

Tap the **Bell** icon to enable Silent Mode, which prevents sound effects and notifications from making any noise.

**7** **App shortcuts**

Tap the **Timer**, **Calculator** or **Camera** button to instantly open these apps. You can also tap and hold to activate features such as timer length and video recording.

## Customize Control Center

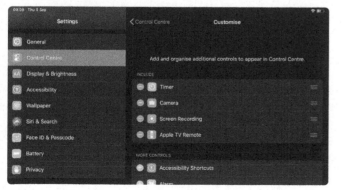

If you want to add additional buttons to Control Center, or remove those that you don't use very often, simply open the **Settings** app and tap **Control Center.** On the following panel you'll find shortcuts to add and remove options. You can also rearrange the options by using the drag buttons to customize Control Center to your exact needs.

# How to use Spotlight

## Search your iPad or quickly access app widgets...

You might not realize, but your iPad knows a lot about your daily schedule and lifestyle. It's continually monitoring your calendar schedule, messages, and more. Don't worry, this data isn't used for nefarious reasons; instead, it's used by the operating system to help you get home on time, meet all your appointments and more; all via the Spotlight screen.

### How to access Spotlight

There are three ways to access the Spotlight screen:

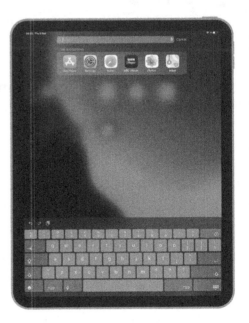

Just raise your iPad or press the **power** button and any new spotlight information will appear on the Lock Screen. These might include new messages, map directions, or your next calendar appointment.

From the Home screen, swipe to the right and the Spotlight widget panel will appear.

From the Home screen, swipe down from the middle of the screen and the Spotlight search panel will appear.

## Edit Spotlight Widgets

By customizing the Spotlight widget panel, you can add your favorite widgets, or clear away any which you don't find helpful. To do this, scroll down to the bottom of the Spotlight panel, then tap the **Edit** button. On the following screen you can add, delete, and reorder widgets to suit your needs.

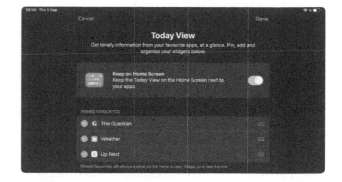

## Show your Spotlight widgets on the Home Screen

If you'd like to see more than just app icons on the Home Screen, then it's possible to add your Spotlight widgets to the left-hand side. Here's how:

**1** Start by opening the **Settings** app. Select **Display & Brightness**, scroll down to the bottom of the panel, then set APP ICON SIZE to **More**.

**2** Next, go back to the Home Screen, swipe towards the right to access Spotlight, scroll down to the bottom and tap **Edit**.

**3** At the top of the edit panel, look for Keep on Home Screen, then toggle it **on**.

**4** Tap **Done** and return to the Home Screen. Rotate your iPad into landscape view and you'll notice your Spotlight widgets appear on the left-side of the screen. Tap on one to view more details, or scroll the widgets upwards to see more of them.

# How to multitask

## Use two apps at once, or watch a video while doing something else...

With the iPad Pro, multitasking between two apps is now a useful and realistic way to work. That's because of the sheer size of the iPad Pro display, which makes it possible to run two full-sized apps at once, watch a video stream while browsing the web, or quickly check your emails while looking through photos. You can also access the Dock at any time, letting you quickly jump between your favorite apps.

There are three multitasking modes included with the iPad Pro: Slide Over, Split View and Picture in Picture. Slide Over lets you quickly open a second app without leaving the one you're currently using; Split View enables you to run two apps at the same time; while Picture in Picture lets you watch a video while still doing other things. Let's take a look at all the multitasking features in a little more detail...

## The Dock

The Dock contains all of your favorite apps. You can always find it at the bottom of the Home screen. You can also access it when you're using an app by swiping up from the bottom of the screen then stopping after an inch or two. To close the Dock swipe it back down or tap in the space above it.

The Dock is split into two parts. On the left side are your favorite apps. You can add up to 8 apps at a time. To do this just visit the Home screen, tap and hold on an app then drag it onto the Dock. On the right side of the Dock are your three most recently opened apps.

## Use Slide Over to quickly control music playback

With Split View on iPad, you can call up a small, windowed view of an app (such as the Music app) and control both apps simultaneously:

**1** Open the first app then slide your finger upwards from the bottom of the screen to access the Dock.

**2** Drag the second app you wish to use from the Dock and slide it towards the left or right side of the screen.

**3** Let go of your finger and the app will hover in place. Slide View is now enabled.

To move a Slide Over app around the screen, place your finger on the top middle part of the app (where you see a grey line) then slide the app to its new position.

To snap a Slide Over app into place, so it can be run in Split View, tap the grey line then slide it upwards.

To dismiss a Slide Over app, simply slide it off the screen to the left or right. The app will still be there, even when you can't see it. You can bring it back by sliding your finger inwards from the side of the screen.

## Use Split View to run two apps at once

With Split View you can run two apps at the same time, here's how it works:

**1** Open the first app then slide your finger upwards from the bottom of the screen to access the Dock.

**2** Drag the second app from the Dock and move it to the far left or right of the screen. You'll see the app "snap" to the side of the screen. Let go and it will now appear as a Split View app.

It's possible to make one app larger than the other using Split View, with 2/3rds of the screen taken up by one app, and 1/3rd by the other. To do this simply tap and drag the thin black line that separates the two apps, then move it left or right.

To swap a Split View app with another, open the Dock by swiping up the screen, then drag an app from the Dock and slide it over the app you wish to replace.

To close Split View, drag the thin black bar that separates the two apps off the screen.

## Use Picture in Picture to watch a video while checking an email

While watching a video in the TV app, or making a FaceTime video call, quickly swipe upwards to go home and the video will scale down to a corner of the display. This helpful way to watch videos on iPad means you can open a second app, check an email, or write a tweet while still watching your favorite TV show.

You can resize the video window by pinching on it, swipe it to the side of the screen to only listen to the audio, or tap on the video then tap the full-screen button to return to your show without any distractions.

## Use drag and drop to move things between apps

Drag and drop is a truly powerful tool on iPad, and it's delightfully simple to use. It works by letting you drag anything from one app to another. It can be an image, a link, a chunk of text... whatever you like. You can even drag multiple items at once to save time. It takes a little practice, but once perfected you'll wonder how you ever lived without this clever feature.

**What can you drag and drop?**
- Nearly anything, such as:
- Contacts
- Phone numbers
- Photos
- Text

## The basics of drag and drop

Let's start by running the Photos app and Notes app in either Split or Slideover view:

1   In the Photos app, tap and hold on a photo. After a moment it will lift off the screen and attach to your finger.

2   Next, slide the photo over to the Notes app. You'll see a small green icon appear when drag and drop is available. Once you see this let go.

3   The photo will now be dropped into place. It's that simple!

# How to drag and drop multiple items

While we're still looking at the Photos and Notes app...

1. **Tap and hold** on a photo, then wait for it to attach to your finger.

2. Tap on another photo and it will also attach to your finger (you might need to use two fingers to do this).

3. You can select as many photos as you wish using this technique.

4. Slide the photos over the Notes app and let go. They will all drop into place!

# How to drag and drop files into other apps

It's possible to drag items into another app that's not in Split or Slideover view. In fact, there are multiple ways you can drag items to another app. Begin by selecting an item (or multiple items), then:

1. Swipe up to go home with your other hand, select the app you wish to move the items too then drop them into place.

2. Use your other hand to swipe up from the bottom of the screen to enable the Dock, select the app then drop the item/s in place.

3. Use four fingers and swipe across the screen to go between earlier apps. When you get to the right app, drop the item/s in place.

# Connect to a Wi-Fi network

Easily connect to home, office, or public Wi-Fi networks...

Connecting to a Wi-Fi network is one of those fundamental tasks that we all must do from time to time. Perhaps you're visiting a friend and would like to hook up to their internet connection, or you might be sat in a coffee shop that offers free Wi-Fi. Here's how to do it:

**1** Open the **Settings** app then tap the **Wi-Fi** option.

**2** If Wi-Fi isn't already turned on then tap the toggle button near the top of the screen.

**3** Select a wireless network, then enter its password if necessary.

**4** Tap the blue **Join** button on the keyboard. If you've entered the password successfully your iPad will automatically join the network.

## Public networks

If the network doesn't require a password, then you can just tap on the Wi-Fi network name and immediately connect. Note, however, that sometimes networks require you to enter personal details via the Safari app before you can freely browse the web. You'll probably come across this situation in coffee shops and airports. Hotels might also request you to enter your hotel room number and a password, the latter of which is typically available from the reception.

## Share a Wi-Fi password

Looking for the Wi-Fi password is always a pain. It's usually hidden on the back of a router, printed on an obscure piece of card or written in small print on a receipt. Over time this becomes less of a problem, as Wi-Fi passwords are stored in your iCloud account, so once you connect to a network all of your devices will automatically join when they come within reach; but nevertheless, those new networks will still appear every now and then.

With the Share Wi-Fi feature, joining wireless networks becomes slightly easier, because you can automatically copy Wi-Fi passwords from one iOS device to another. Here's how it works:

**1** Enter the range of a new WiFi network.

**2** Place your iPad near an unlocked iOS device that's already connected to the Wi-Fi network.

**3** Your iPad will automatically ask the other device for the Wi-Fi password.

**4** If the owner of the other device agrees to the request, then you'll receive the password automatically and instantly connect.

# iCloud

## Learn what iCloud is all about...

iCloud enables you to sync all of your images, videos, music, apps, contacts, calendars and much more across your iPhone and Mac or PC. This means you can snap a photo on your iPad then see it automatically appear on your iPhone, Mac, or Apple TV. It means you can purchase a song, movie or TV show in iTunes, and see it appear on all of your Apple devices. It means you can start writing a document on your Mac, edit it on your iPad, and see the changes appear across both devices. You can also backup your iPad wirelessly, see where your friends are on a map, sync bookmarks and much more.

## Photos

Any photos taken on your iPad are wirelessly uploaded to iCloud, then automatically downloaded onto your other iOS devices, Mac and/or PC. So you can take a photo during the day on your iPad, then get home and view it larger on your Mac, all without having to sync or use wires.

## iCloud Drive

iCloud Drive automatically saves all your documents created in Pages, Keynote, Numbers and Notes, then wirelessly beams them to your other devices. So if you're writing a letter or creating a presentation on your Mac, you'll be able to continue editing it on your iPad or iPhone without having to worry about saving it or transferring the file. Edits are automatically updated across all of your devices too. It works like magic. To access all the files in your iCloud Drive, simply open the **Files** app then select **iCloud Drive**.

## Find My iPhone (for iPad)

If you can't find your iPad, Find My iPhone will enable you to track it through iCloud. By signing into your iCloud account, either from www.icloud.com or another iPhone, you can see your devices on a map, set a passcode lock, remotely wipe them or send a message to the screen. You can also enable Lost Mode, whereby the device is automatically locked, a message with a contact appears on the screen and the device automatically tracks where it's been and reports it back to Find My iPhone.

## Safari

iCloud automatically saves your bookmarks, Reading Lists and open tabs. So if you're reading a lengthy web article on your Mac but need to dash, you can continue reading it at a later time on your iPad. To do this open **Safari** on your iPad, tap on the **Tabs** button in the top-right corner, then scroll down to see every tab open on all of your Apple devices.

## Backup

iCloud automatically backs up your iPad when it's plugged into a power source and connected to the web over Wi-Fi. iCloud backs up the following things: music, movies, TV shows, apps, books, photos and videos in the Camera Roll, device settings, app data, ringtones, app organization and messages. And if you buy a new iPad, you can restore all of the above by using an existing iCloud backup.

# Display settings

## Learn how to adjust the display to meet your needs...

The display of your iPad is its most crucial component because it's the one you spend the most time prodding, poking, and stroking.

You might not know it, but there are some essential settings available for the iPad which let you adjust the screen to suit your needs better. You can play around with the brightness, enable True Tone, and capture what's on the screen to share with others...

### Adjust the brightness

If you'd like to adjust the brightness of the display, just swipe down from the top-right corner of the screen to access Control Center, then slide the brightness slider up or down. You can also tap and hold on the slider to enable a larger version that's easier to control.

### Adjust Auto-Brightness

By default your iPad will automatically adjust the brightness of the display to match the conditions of your environment; so if you're in a dark room, the screen will dim accordingly.

To turn this off or on, go to **Settings > Accessibility > Display & Text Size** and turn **Auto-Brightness** off.

### Adjust the Auto-Timer

If you'd like to adjust how long it takes until your iPad locks, go to **Settings > Display & Brightness > Auto-Lock**, where you'll find several settings that range from 1 minute to never.

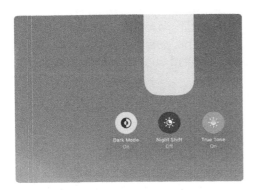

### Disable True Tone

True Tone is a brilliant feature that adjusts the screen ambience to match the environment around you. So if you're sitting in a room with yellowish light, the screen will subtly change to suit the environment.

If you prefer the screen to always look pure white, open the **Settings** app and go to **Display & Brightness,** then toggle **True Tone** off. You can also disable True Tone from Control Center. Just tap and hold on the brightness slider, then tap the **True Tone** button.

## Take a screenshot

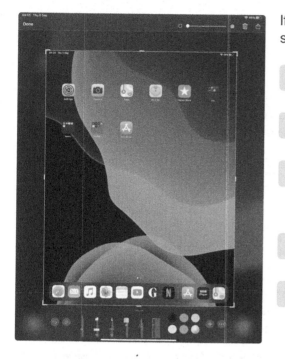

If you want to share something interesting on your screen then taking a screenshot of it is a great way to do this. Here's how it works:

**1** Press the **Power** button and **Volume Up** buttons at the same time to capture the screen.

**2** You'll see a thumbnail of the screenshot minimize and snap to the bottom left corner.

**3** Leave the thumbnail alone for a few seconds and it will disappear and save the screenshot to the Photos app. You can also swipe the thumbnail to the left to quickly save it.

**4** Tap on the thumbnail and you can annotate it or delete it.

**5** **Press firmly** on the thumbnail and you can easily share it with friends and contacts, print it or even create a watch face.

## Create a video recording of the screen

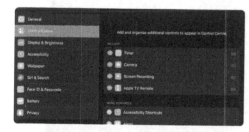

Start by adding the Screen Recording widget to Control Center. To do this go to **Settings > Control Center > Customize Controls** then add **Screen Recording**.

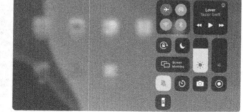

Close the Settings app and swipe down from the top-right corner to enable Control Center.

Tap the **Screen Recording** button (it looks like the outline of a circle with a dot in the middle) and after three seconds the recording will begin.

Tap the **red pill bar** at the top of the screen to stop the recording.

To capture audio, press and hold on the **Screen Recording** button within Control Center, then tap **Microphone Audio**.

# Toggle Dark Mode

## Give your apps an evocative new look...

With Dark Mode you can turn to the dark side by giving all the default apps an evocative new look. Basically, whites become black, folder backgrounds and the Dock take on a smokey look, and even the default wallpapers supplied by Apple take on a darker look.

### Enable Dark Mode

There are two ways you can turn on (or off) Dark Mode:

**1** Access Control Center, tap and hold on the brightness slider, then tap the **Appearance** button in the bottom-left corner.

**2** Open the **Settings** app, select **Display & Brightness**, then tap the **Dark** option at the top of the screen.

# Dark Mode comparisons...

## Lock screen

## Photos

## Maps

## Notes

## Music

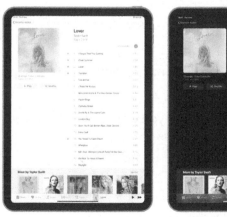

## App Store

# How to manage Notifications

## Discover how to manage notifications...

However you use your iPad, you're going to receive notifications on a regular basis. Notifications usually appear when you have a new message, or if an app wants to get your attention. If your iPad is locked, then the notification will appear as a bubble on the Lock Screen. If you're using your device when the notification arrives, then it will appear as a floating panel at the top of the screen. If an app wants to get your attention, then you might see a red dot above its icon on the Home screen.

If there's one annoying aspect about receiving notifications on an iPad, it's that you can't simply ignore them. Try to do that, and they'll only end up in the Notification Center, forever awaiting an action from yourself. Similarly, if you try and ignore that little red dot above an app icon, and it'll never go away. Thankfully, you can customize, hide, and even disable notifications from individual apps...

## Change how notifications appear

To change an alert style for a notification, go to **Settings > Notifications**, then select an app. Here are some of the alert styles you can choose from:

- **Allow Notifications:** Toggle on to receive notifications from the app you selected.

- **Banners:** Choose how you want notifications to appear when your iPad is unlocked. Tap **Temporary** to display alerts for a short period of time, or tap **Persistent** to have alerts stay on the screen until you act on it.

- **Sounds:** Toggle sound alerts for when you receive a notification.

- **Show on Lock Screen:** Turn on to see notifications on your Lock screen.

- **Show in History:** See previous notifications from the app you selected.

- **Show Previews:** Choose what you want to see when you get a notification, like a text message.

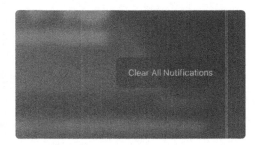

### Clear all your notifications at once

If you have a stack of notifications waiting for you in Notification Center, then you can clear them all at once by tapping and holding on the small **X** button:

### Interact with notifications

If a notification appears while you're using your iPad, pull it down from the top of the screen using your finger to interact with it. For example, if you get a message, pull the notification down and you'll be able to send a reply without going into the Messages app.

### View grouped notifications

When you receive multiple notifications from the same source, then these will appear as a "stack" of notifications on the Lock Screen. By tapping on this stack, you can expand it. You can also swipe across a group of notifications to manage them, view them or clear them all away.

## Configure notifications

If you receive an unwanted notification from an app or person, then you can customize how any further notifications from this source will appear. To do this, **tap and hold** on a notification, tap the **options** button (it looks like three dots) and a Manage panel will slide up from the bottom of the screen, with two large buttons: Deliver Quietly, and Turn Off...

- **Delivery Quietly**
  Press **Deliver Quietly,** and any further notifications from this source will only appear inside Notification Center, so you won't see any more Lock Screen notifications from this source, banners, app icon badges, or hear any sounds.

- **Turn Off**
  Press **Turn Off**, and you'll switch off all future notifications.

If you want to adjust notifications with more detail, then there's a **Settings** button at the bottom of the panel.

# Talk to Siri

## Take command of your very own assistant...

Imagine Siri as your very own personal assistant. He (or she depending on your country of origin) can make FaceTime calls for you, dictate emails and messages, make a restaurant reservation, remind you to do things, tell you about movies, make jokes, and much more.

Siri isn't perfect, however. It can't remember interactions from the past, it relies on hearing your voice in a clear manner, and it needs a connection to the internet to work. If you're aware of these limitations and don't mind the odd false request, then Siri can save time and even be a little fun to use.

To enable Siri just hold down on the **Power** button. After two seconds you'll hear Siri chime. You can now begin issuing commands, or if you're unsure, stay quiet and after a moment or two you'll see some of the things you can ask Siri.

### Speak to Siri

Say out loud, "*What's the weather like today?*" Siri will automatically look for a weather report then tell you what it's going to be like. It's that simple to use Siri. When you're finished with Siri, press the **Power** button to return to where you were before.

### Dictate text with Siri

If you'd like Siri to dictate a message or email, then simply say something like, "*Tell Noah I'll be late*". Siri will automatically create a new message or email to the recipient that says 'I'll be late home tonight'.

### Activate Siri via voice command

It's possible to activate Siri by simply saying "*Hey Siri.*" After you hear the recognizable Siri chime, say a command out loud (such as "tell me the time") and Siri will respond – all without your touch. To enable this feature, go to **Settings > Siri & Search**, and turn on **Listen for "Hey Siri".**

# Things you can ask Siri...

# Accounts, emails, and passwords

Learn how to add your email account, calendar events, and passwords...

As you use your iPad to do day to day things, such as checking emails, adding calendar events, or logging into websites, then you're going to start accumulating login details, accounts, and passwords. On this page you'll learn the basics of adding accounts and personal details. Most of it happens automatically, and once you've added an account you'll be able to start emailing friends and family, check your calendar for events, plus much more.

## Add your email account

Start by opening the **Settings** app, then tap on **Passwords & Accounts**.

Tap on **Add Account**.

Select your email provider. If your email address ends with "gmail.com", then tap on Google. If it ends with "hotmail.com", select the Outlook option. You get the idea.

Your iPad will ask for the username and password associated with your email account. Simply enter these and tap **Next**.

Your device will verify your mail account details. Once the process has completed you can choose whether you wish to sync mail, contacts and notes.

## Add calendar events you've saved to Gmail, Outlook, or a personal account

If you've ever used a Gmail or Outlook account to add calendar events, then your iPad can automatically load these from the internet and add them to the Calendar app. Similarly, when you add a new event or modify an existing one, your iPad will sync the changes to your account on the internet. This means if you log into your account using a web browser or another computer, all the changes you made on your iPad will appear there too.

### If you've already added your Apple, Gmail, Outlook, or Yahoo account...

**1** Start by opening the **Settings** app, then tap on **Passwords & Accounts**.

**2** Tap on your account.

**3** On the following screen, toggle the **Calendar** button on, so it appears green.

### If you're adding a new account...

**1** Start by opening the **Settings** app, then tap on **Passwords & Accounts**.

**2** Tap on the **Add Account** option, then select your email provider from the list displayed on-screen.

**3** Your iPad will ask for the username and password associated with your email account. Simply enter these and tap **Next**.

**4** Your device will verify your mail account details. Once the process has completed you can choose whether you wish to sync mail, contacts and notes.

## Look for a password

Whenever you login into a website and enter a username, email address, or password, your iPad will ask if you would like to save these details on the device. If you agree, the next time you go back to the website and try to log in, your iPad will automatically offer to enter your details. It's a great time-saving feature, and it also means you don't have to remember every single password you've ever entered.

Sometimes you might need to take a look at these passwords and login details. Perhaps you're using someone else's computer and can't remember your password, or maybe you've accidentally saved multiple login details for a site and want to tidy them up. Here's how you can access every password and account saved on your iPad in a few steps...

**1** Open the **Settings** app, then tap on **Passwords and Accounts**. At the top of the screen, choose **Website & App Passwords**.

**2** Your iPad will automatically scan your face, to make sure it's you that's accessing your personal details.

**3** You'll then see a list of every website you've ever logged into.

**4** You can search for a website, username, email address, or password, by using the search field at the top of the screen.

**5** You can also tap on individual accounts to see the details you've saved.

**6** To delete a set of details, swipe across the account from right to left, then tap the red **Delete** button.

# Type like a Pro

## Become a master at typing on the iPad keyboard...

The software keyboard built into your iPad is amazing in several ways. It guesses what word you're trying to write, then automatically finishes it for you. It rotates with the screen to make typing easier. It can detect up to 10 fingertips to make typing quicker. You can hold down a key to see more options, plus much more. If you're new to typing on a glass screen then give it some time. The first few days might be frustrating as you work out how best to hold your iPad. Personally, I like to hold my iPad Pro using both hands in the portrait orientation, and use my thumbs to type each key (yes, they just reach!) However, for long periods of typing, I prefer to rest my iPad horizontally on a surface, then type using both hands. Once you're comfortable typing, here are some tips for making the most out of the iPad's keyboard...

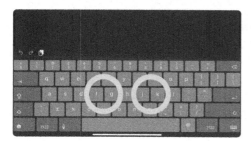

### Quickly select a word

By double-tapping two fingers on the keyboard you can quickly select a word. Double-tap then drag your finger and you'll be able to select multiple words or sentences.

### Slide to type numbers or capitals

You can easily add a number by holding your finger on the **123** key, then sliding it to a number that appears. This slide-to-type method also works with capital letters.

### Create your own shortcuts

With shortcuts enabled, you can type "omw" and your iPad will automatically write "On my way!" To create your own shortcuts go to **Settings > General > Keyboard > Text Replacement**.

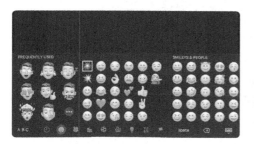

### Use Emojis

You can quickly include an emoji with a message by tapping the Emoji button in the bottom-left corner of the keyboard.

### Include a Memoji Sticker

You can also include your very own personalized Memoji sticker with a message. Just tap the **Memoji** button above the keyboard. To learn how to create your own Memoji, jump to the Messages chapter on page 86.

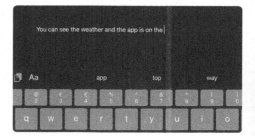

### Predictive Text

Predictive Text attempts to guess the next word you want to type. To see it in action, open the **Messages** app and begin to reply to a recipient. As you enter each letter, a series of words will appear above the keyboard. To use a word just tap on it.

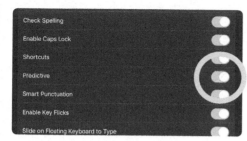

### Hide the predictive text panel

If you'd like to hide or enable the predictive text panel just open the **Settings** app and go to **General > Keyboard** then toggle **Predictive** on or off.

### Accents and extra keys

To add accents, extra letters and punctuation, **tap and hold** on a key. You'll see extra options and letters appear above your finger. To select one, simply drag your finger to it then let go.

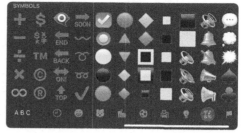

### Add a trademark symbol

To find the trademark, copyright and registered symbols, open the **Emoji** keyboard then tap the character button that's second from the right. Swipe through the emojis a few times and eventually you'll see the trademark, copyright and registered symbols.

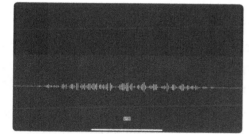

### Dictate in real-time

To see your words appear as text in real-time, tap the **Microphone** key next to the spacebar then begin to talk out loud. You'll see your words appear on the screen in real-time.

### Format text with the shortcut keys

As you use the iPad's keyboard for typing and entering text you'll probably notice the shortcut keys above they keyboard (if they don't appear then swipe the small grey bar above the keyboard upwards). Usually these enable you to cut, copy, paste, format text and attach images or files with just a tap of a button, but some apps may add further shortcuts.

### Easily move the text cursor

If you'd like to quickly move the text cursor to another word or line, **press and hold** on the spacebar then use it as a trackpad with your finger.

### Shrink the keyboard

Pinch on the keyboard with two fingers to shrink it down. You can now slide it to the edge of the screen and type one-handed.

### Swipe to type

While using the smaller keyboard, you can also swipe from key-to-key to type words.

# How to copy, paste, and select text

Discover how to copy something then paste it somewhere else...

Copying and pasting is a great way to move text or content from one app to another. For example, you could copy your address from Contacts and paste it into Safari, or copy a photo and then paste it into an email. The options are endless.

## Copy and paste gestures

It takes some practice, but the best way to copy and paste text is to use a series of three-finger gesures. Start by selecting a piece of text (to do this just tap and hold on the text), then perform one of the following gestures:

- **Copy**: Perform a three-finger pinch.
- **Cut**: Three-finger double pinch.
- **Paste**: Three-finger pinch out.
- **Undo**: Swipe left with three fingers.
- **Redo**: Swipe right with three fingers.
- **Access a shortcut menu:** Three-finger tap.

When you successfully use one of the three-finger gestures you'll see a confirmation at the top of your screen. Here's how it looks:

**Copy text without a gesture**

Find a source of text on your iPad, perhaps your phone number in Contacts. **Tap and hold** your finger on the number, let go when the magnifying glass appears, then choose **Copy** from the pop-up button.

**Paste text without a gesture**

Next, close Contacts and open the Notes app. Create a new note by tapping the **plus** icon, then **tap and hold** on the empty note and choose **Paste**. Your phone number will appear in the new note.

**Copy images**

To copy an image from the Photos app, open it, tap the **Share** button in the top corner, then choose **Copy**. You can now paste this image into a new email, SMS or iMessage.

**Cursor navigation**

You can pick up the cursor and drag it somewhere else.

**Multiselect text**

Quickly select a block of text by dragging your finger across it.

**Intelligent text selection**

You can select a word with a double tap, a sentence with three taps, and a whole paragraph with four taps.

# How to use the Share sheet

Learn how to share something with other people or perform actions...

There's a lot you can do with a photo on your iPad. You can edit it (which we cover in the Photos chapter), share it with friends, hide it, duplicate it, print it, or even save it to the Files app. The same goes for other things on your iPad, like notes, reminders, and web pages. You can share all of these things (and more) by using the Share sheet, which you can access by pressing the Share button. It's usually tucked away in a corner, and it looks like this:

## Share something with a friend

When you tap the Share button, you'll see contact suggestions near the top of the panel. These are based on your recent activity with friends and family, so you might see a shortcut to email something, attach it to a message or AirDrop it from one Apple device to another.

## App shortcuts

Below the contact suggestions panel are a series of app shortcuts. If you decide to share a photo, you might see shortcuts for sending it within a message, posting it on Facebook, or attaching it within a note.

## Other shortcuts

Scroll down the Share sheet, and you'll find a wide range of context-sensitive shortcuts. These are based on the thing you're sharing, so if it's a photo, you'll see shortcuts to hide it, duplicate it, or even make a watch face for your Apple Watch. Decide to share a web page, and you'll see shortcuts for adding a bookmark, finding a piece of on-page text and copying the URL.

# Use AirDrop to share files

Send photos or files to friends nearby...

Have you ever wanted to share a photo, note, or video with someone else in the same room? So long as they also have an iPhone, iPad, or Mac, then it's possible to wirelessly transfer something with just a few taps. It works using a combination of Wi-Fi and Bluetooth, and there's no setup required. As a result it's never been quicker or easier to share files with friends, family and colleagues.

## Enable AirDrop

To turn on AirDrop go to **Settings** > **General** > **AirDrop**. You can also use Control Center. To do this open Control Center, tap and hold on the box in the top-left corner, then tap **AirDrop**.

## Share a file

AirDrop is now active. To share a file, open a photo, note, web page, or anything else with share capabilities, then tap the blue **Share** button at the bottom of the screen. You'll see the AirDrop button near the middle of the Share sheet. Tap this and you'll see anyone nearby with AirDrop enabled. To share the file with them, just tap on their face or name.

## Choose who to share files with

By default, only people saved in your Contacts book can share files with you. To change this setting and let anyone send you a file:

1   Open Control Center.

2   Tap and hold on the top-left box.

3   Tap the **AirDrop** button.

4   Choose whether anyone can send you files, just your Contacts, or turn AirDrop off.

# Use Handoff to work between devices

## Start something on your iPad then continue it on your iPhone or Mac...

Most people won't have heard about Handoff. It's a rather clever feature which lets you start something on your iPad, then continue it on an iPhone or Mac.

Take writing an email for example, you might begin to compose a message on your iPhone, then sit down at your desk and finish the email on your Mac. Or maybe you start reading a web page on your iPhone then continue it on an iPad with a bigger screen. Here's how it works:

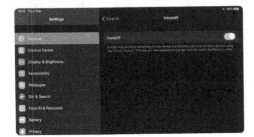

### Turn Handoff on

To enable Handoff on your iPad, go to **Settings** > **General** > **Handoff**, then toggle the **Handoff** switch on.

On a Mac, open **System Preferences**, click **General**, then ensure **Allow Handoff between this Mac and your iCloud devices** is ticked.

### Jump from iPad to Mac

It's easy to swap tasks between an iPad and Mac. Take reading a web page for example. When you open a web page on your iPad, a Safari icon will appear on the left-side of the Dock on the Mac. Just click on this icon to open the same webpage on your Mac.

This same process goes for composing Notes, Emails and Messages, or adding Calendar and Contact entries.

### Jump from iPhone to iPad

If you'd like to continue a task on your iPad, begin writing, adding, or reading content on your iPhone, then turn on your iPad and go to the Home screen. You'll see an icon on the right-side of the Dock for the relevant app, with a small iPhone above it. Tap on this icon and you'll open the content from your iPhone, on your iPad.

### Requirements

Handoff requires a Mac running Yosemite or later to talk to your iPad, so you'll need a 2012 iMac or later, MacBook Air, MacBook Pro, or late 2013 Mac Pro. Additionally, you'll need to have Bluetooth enabled on every device, and they all need to be approximately 30 feet or less from each other.

# Use your iPad as a second monitor

Extend or mirror your Mac's monitor onto your iPad...

If you're fortunate enough to own both a Mac and an iPad, then it's possible to use your iPad as a second monitor, effectively giving you extra space to run desktop apps or keep documents and files. Alternatively, you can mirror your Mac's screen onto the iPad, enabling you to use it as a miniature Mac when you're away from the desk. Here's how it works:

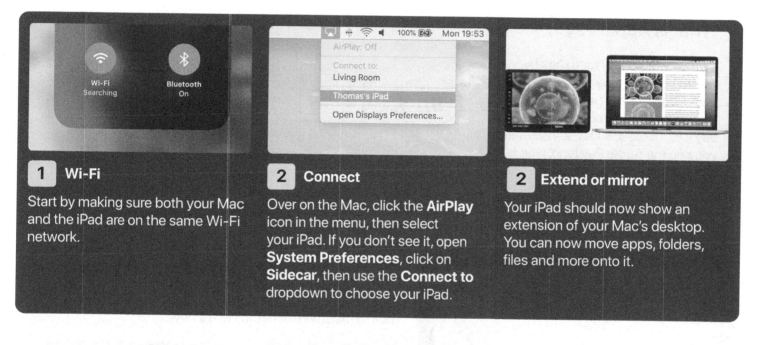

**1  Wi-Fi**

Start by making sure both your Mac and the iPad are on the same Wi-Fi network.

**2  Connect**

Over on the Mac, click the **AirPlay** icon in the menu, then select your iPad. If you don't see it, open **System Preferences**, click on **Sidecar**, then use the **Connect to** dropdown to choose your iPad.

**2  Extend or mirror**

Your iPad should now show an extension of your Mac's desktop. You can now move apps, folders, files and more onto it.

**The sidebar**

The sidebar displays commonly used controls on the side of your iPad screen. You'll find shortcuts to the Command key, Shift, and other modifier keys. This enables you to choose essential commands with your finger or Apple Pencil, instead of a keyboard.

**The Touch Bar**

The latest Macbook Pro includes a Touch Bar on its keyboard which displays commonly-used shortcuts. The same Touch Bar appears at the bottom of the iPad's screen when using Sidecar. If you don't see it, just drag a window or app onto the iPad's display.

**Additional Settings**

You can customize Sidecar by going to **System Preferences** on your Mac, then **Sidecar**. On the following panel, you'll see options to enable or disable the sidebar and Touch Bar or enable double-tap on the Apple Pencil. Toggle this on, and you can perform custom actions when you double-tap on the side of your Apple Pencil.

# Use Apple Pay to buy things

## Leave your wallet in the drawer...

Apple Pay is pretty remarkable. You can use it to pay for apps and music with your iPad, or buy items online without entering your credit card details.

### What is Apple Pay?

It's a way of paying for things by holding your iPhone or Apple Watch near a contactless payment terminal. On an iPad you can use it online to pay for goods, or within apps when you see the Apple Pay logo, which looks like this:

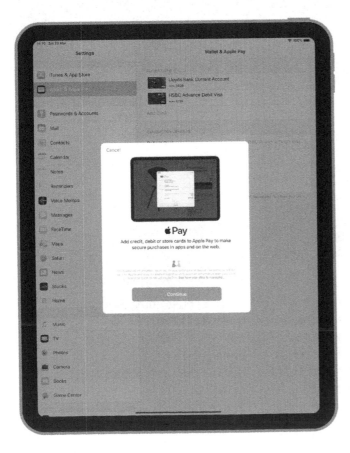

### How to enable Apple Pay on your iPad

The first step is to add a credit or debit card, of which you can hold a maximum of eight. Here's how:

**1** Open the **Settings** app, go to **Wallet & Apple Pay**, then follow the steps to add a card. If you're trying to add a card which already exists withing your Apple ID account, then you'll only need to enter its security code.

**2** Tap **Next** and your bank will authorize and add your card. If your bank needs more details you can add these later via **Settings > Wallet & Apple Pay**.

### Use Apple Pay online

If you're using Safari and see the Apple Pay button at the checkout, just tap the button to make the purchase immediately.

### Use Apple Pay in an app

If you're using an app and see the Apple Pay logo, you might need to toggle a setting that enables Apple Pay first — the app will let you know. Once enabled, tap the **Apple Pay** button, ensure all the details are correct, then use Face ID to confirm your identity.

### Choose which card to use

The card linked to your Apple ID will automatically be the default card for Apple Pay, but you can change the default card via **Settings** > **Wallet & Apple Pay** > **Default Card**.

### See your recent transactions

Every time you use Apple Pay the last few transactions will be stored as virtual receipts on your iPad. To see these open the **Settings** app, select **Wallet & Apple Pay**, tap on the credit/debit card of choice and any payments will appear in the Transactions section.

### Remove a debit or credit card

Open the **Settings** app, select **Wallet & Apple Pay**, tap on the card you wish to remove then tap the **Remove Card** button that appears at the bottom of the screen.

# Use AirPlay to stream content to a TV

## Send video and music to your TV, or even your iPad's entire screen...

With AirPlay you can wirelessly stream content to an Apple TV, or play music over AirPlay speakers such as HomePod. All you need to do is connect your iPad to the same Wi-Fi connection shared with your AirPlay devices; there are no complicated configurations to set up, all the hard work is done for you.

**What you can stream to an AirPlay device:**

- Music and Beats 1 Radio

**What you can stream to an Apple TV:**

- Movies and videos
- Music and Beats 1 Radio
- Photos and slideshows
- Third-party video-based apps (such as Netflix or BBC iPlayer)
- Your entire iPad display

## Stream content to your Apple TV

**1** Connect your iPad to the same Wi-Fi connection as the Apple TV.

**2** Swipe down from the top-right corner of the screen to access Control Center.

**3** You will see a wireless icon in the top-right corner of the playback control window. Tap it to choose the Apple TV or AirPlay device.

**4** If you've never connected your device to the Apple TV before, enter the 4-character passcode that appears on the TV.

To turn off AirPlay, return to Control Center, tap the playback controls window, tap **AirPlay** then select your device. You can also press the **Back** button on the Apple TV remote.

# Stream a video you're watching to an Apple TV

While watching a video tap the screen to access playback controls, then tap the **AirPlay** button. In the pop-up window, select the Apple TV and you'll start to stream the video.

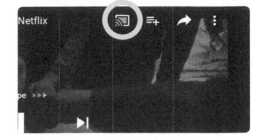

## Mirror your iPad display

Want to share your iPad screen on your Apple TV? It's easy, just swipe down from the top-right corner of the screen to access Control Center, tap **Screen Mirroring** then choose the Apple TV.

Your iPad will immediately begin mirroring its display. While your screen is being mirrored everything you do on the iPad will appear on-screen, including messages, websites and apps. Note how the images rotates into landscape mode when your turn your device on its side. Also note, that if you view a photo or video while mirroring it will appear full-screen on the TV. To turn off mirroring, just bring Control Center back up, tap the white **Apple TV** button, then tap **Stop Mirroring**. Alternatively, lock your iPad via the **power** button and the stream will end, or if you have the Apple TV remote to hand press the **Back** button.

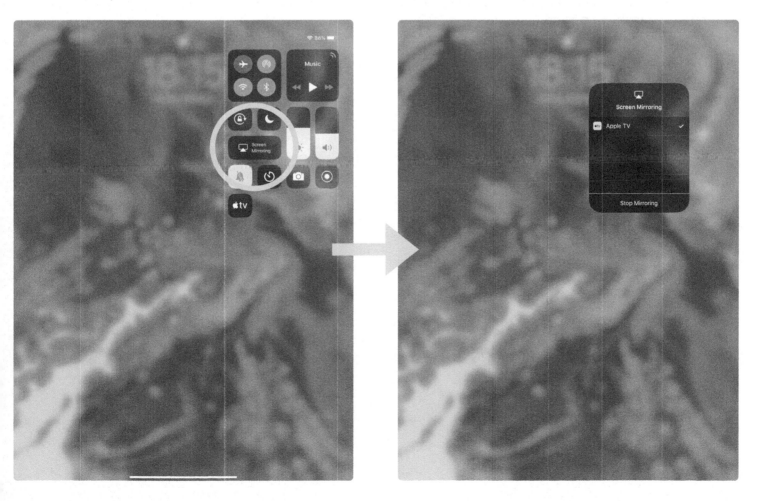

# Apps

Every app on your iPad transform it into a completely different tool. The Safari app lets you browse and search the web, the Camera app enables you to take stunning photos, while FaceTime lets you make video calls to friends and family. These are just a few of the millions of apps available for your iPad.

This next few pages will explain how to use and manage these apps. You'll learn how to open and close apps, organize them into folders, and even explore the App Store.

# The basics of using apps

Learn what an app is, how to open and close apps, plus more...

Each app on your iPad specializes in a particular task, so if you want to take a photo, just tap on the Camera app; and if you want to send a text message, then tap on the Messages app. You can never break your iPad by opening the wrong app, so feel free to open each app to see what it does and how it works.

### Open an app

You can open any app on your iPad by lightly tapping on its icon. Just a quick tap of your fingertip is all that's needed.

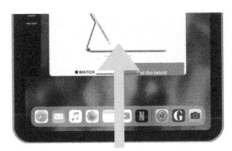

### Close an app

When you're ready to close an app and return to the home screen, just swipe upwards from the bottom of the screen.

### Force an app to quit

If you're using an app and it stops working, swipe upwards from the bottom of the screen then stop after a few inches. You'll see a grid of recently opened apps appear. To force quit the app you were just using, slide it upwards off the top of the screen.

### Delete an app

If you've downloaded an app but want to remove it, simply tap and hold on the app icon, wait a moment, then tap the **cross** button that appears when the app starts to wiggle.

### Tap and hold for options

You can **tap and hold** on most things on your iPad to access additional options, so tap and hold on an app and you can rearrange it or quickly jump to something within the app.

### Create a folder of apps

Simply **tap and hold** on an app, wait until it starts to jiggle, then drag it on top of another app. This will create a folder of apps. You can rename a folder by tapping and holding on its name.

# Built-in apps you need to know about

Discover what each app does and how to find out more...

Although the majority of apps are named clearly -- such as Photos -- there are a few which might cause you to scratch your head. Take Safari, for example. It doesn't teach you about the many animals and activities you can expect to find on a wild safari trip, but rather it lets you browse and search the web. Here's a quick overview of each build-in app and where to find out more...

## Internet and communication apps:

### Safari

You can use the Safari app to browse and search the internet.

**Visit page 94 for more...**

### Mail

Check your emails, organize your inbox and send emails.

**Visit page 98 for more...**

### Messages

Send text messages or share photos and videos with friends and family.

**Visit page 102 for more...**

### FaceTime

Make free video calls on your iPad to anyone with an iPhone, iPad, or Mac.

**Visit page 110 for more...**

## Useful apps:

### Notes

Quickly jot down notes and ideas. You can also share them with friends.

**Visit page 156 for more...**

### Reminders

Create reminders and do-to lists, then assign them to dates and locations.

**Visit page 154 for more...**

### Maps

Explore the entire world on your iPad, with 3D maps, navigation and more.

**Visit page 144 for more...**

### Files

Manage your files and folders stored in iCloud, across multiple devices.

**Visit page 160 for more...**

**Continued across the page...**

## Photos and Media apps:

### Music

Listen to millions of tracks and albums on Apple Music.

**Visit page 136 for more...**

### App Store

Browse and download a nearly limitless number of unique apps.

**Visit page 82 for more...**

### Photos

View and edit all the photos and videos stored on your iPad.

**Visit page 122 for more...**

### Books

Explore a massive library of digital books, audiobooks and comics.

### News

Catch up with the latest news and magazines from around the world.

**Visit page 148 for more...**

### iTunes Store

Purchase singles and albums on the iTunes Store.

### TV

Stream or purchase movies and TV shows.

**Visit page 140 for more...**

### Camera

You guessed it - this app lets you capture photos and videos with your iPad.

**Visit page 114 for more...**

### Podcasts

Discover free audio stories, then stream or download them to your iPad.

## Other helpful apps:

### Shortcuts

Create advanced shortcuts which can be initiated using Siri.

**Visit page 152 for more...**

### Stocks

Monitor the leading stocks and news.

**Visit page 150 for more...**

# Remove default apps

How to get rid of the apps you never use...

Even the staunchest Apple fan will admit that some of the default apps on iPad are unnecessary. After all, not everyone is a stock analyst, and we don't all use the Find Friends app to check the whereabouts of our friends and family. It's possible to organize any unnecessary apps into a specific folder then forget about them, or alternatively, you can delete these apps and forget about them entirely. To do this simply tap and hold the app icon that you'd like to remove, then when it starts to wiggle tap the **X** button. You'll see a warning that any local data and app settings will be removed too. If you're happy to proceed tap **Remove** and the app will vanish from your screen.

## Here are the default apps you can remove...

- Reminders
- Stocks
- Calendar
- Contacts
- Facetime
- Find My Friends
- Home
- iBooks
- iCloud Drive
- iTunes Store
- Mail
- Maps
- Music
- News
- Notes
- Podcasts

There are some downsides to removing default apps. For example, if you delete the Mail app then tap an email address within Safari, you'll see a pop-up window which suggests you restore the Mail app.

## Restore a deleted default app

Wondering how you can restore a deleted app such as Notes, Stocks or Find Friends? It's easy, just open the **App Store**, search for the app you'd like to restore then tap the **iCloud** button. In an instant (remember these apps aren't actually deleted from your iPad) the app will be back on the Home Screen and ready to use.

# The App Store

## Discover an unlimited number of amazing apps for your iPad...

Your iPad is a pretty amazing tablet straight from the box, with a great web browser, note-taking app and photo editor; but if you'd like to do something specific, such as watch Netflix, make a Zoom video call, or play a video game, then you'll need to visit the App Store where there are millions more apps to discover.

Think of the App Store as a shopping mall, but for apps. To find it, look for this icon:

Open the App Store, and it's hard not to be overwhelmed by the sheer number of apps, tools, and games available. You'll initially see highlighted apps for the day. This is curated by a team within Apple, and they usually handpick some of the most inventive and fun apps out there. Look at the bottom of the screen, and you'll see shortcuts to the latest games, apps, Apple Arcade (a subscription service focused around games), and a search shortcut which lets you look for a specific app.

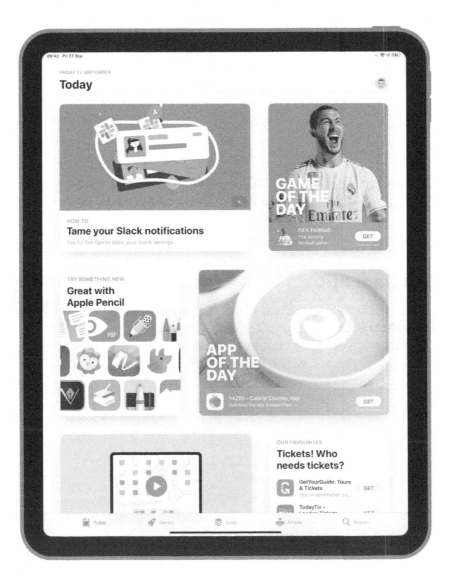

## How to install an app

To install an app, just tap the **GET** button if it's a free app, or the **price** button if it's a paid app.

After you've entered your Apple ID password, the app will be added to the Home screen of your iPad.

**GET**

## In-app purchases

Wondering why that amazing-looking app is free? Chances are it has in-app purchases. Typically an app might charge you to unlock its best features, while an in-app purchase in a game might unlock extra levels.

If an app includes in-app purchases the text "In-App Purchases" will be displayed below the Get button.

**GET**

In-App Purchases

## Get support for an app

If you're having a problem with an app then you'll find support details within the App Store. To find it, locate the app in the App Store, scroll down to the Reviews section, then tap the **App Support** button. Tap on this and you'll be taken to the developers support page on their website. This means the Safari app will take over the screen while you look for support.

## Turn off automatic app updates

Getting the latest version of an app is nearly always a great thing, but there might be times when you don't want apps to automatically update. To turn off automatic updates, go to **Settings** > **iTunes & App Store**, then under **Automatic Download**s, toggle off the **Updates** switch. Apps will no longer update themselves.

## How to review an app

★★★★☆

Want to tell others about how great (or terrible) an app is? First make sure you've already downloaded the app, then head over to its page on the App Store, scroll down to the Reviews section, then tap **Write a Review**.

While writing a review you'll need to create a nickname, rate the app out of five stars, and give the review a title. Keep the title short and descriptive, because the majority of visitors to the App Store only read review titles as they scroll through the page.

# Essential social media apps

## Keep in touch with friends and family...

With its large pin-sharp display, the iPad is a great way to make video calls to friends and family. It's also helpful for sharing photos and writing heartfelt messages to loved ones. To get you started, here are a few social media apps used by millions around the world. You can find them by opening the App Store then using the search feature:

### Facebook
Social Networking
★★★☆☆ 46K

The number one social media platform in the world. The Facebook app doesn't fully take advantage of the iPad's large display (there are borders down each side of the newsfeed), but it's nevertheless a key social media app to keep installed.

**FREE**

### Messenger
Text, audio and video calls
Editors' Choice

You'll need a Facebook account to use Messenger, but once signed up, you can send messages to friends and family and even make free video calls.

**FREE**

### Instagram
Photo & Video
★★★★★ 2.5M

Share photos and videos with others around the world. Where Instagram differs from other social media platforms is that it enables you to follow celebrities - not just your friends and family.

**FREE**

### TikTok - Make Your Day
Real People. Real Videos.
★★★★★ 627K

TikTok is focused entirely around short video clips, mostly themed around dance, lip-sync, comedy, and upcoming talent. With its focus on fast-paced entertainment, it's easily possible to lose an entire evening scrolling through silly video clips.

**FREE**

### Pinterest: Lifestyle Ideas
Healthy recipes & home design
★★★★★ 345K

For the creative type, Pinterest can provide a continuous source of inspiration. It enables to share and discover recipes, home ideas, artwork, style inspiration and more.

**FREE**

### Twitter
Live news, sports, and chat
★★★★★ 433K

With a limit of just 280 characters, Twitter is focused entirely on efficient communication. It's used by presidents, businesses, celebrities, and regular folks alike, and stands alongside Facebook as one of the biggest social media networks on the planet.

**FREE**

### Reddit
Find your community
★★★★★ 132K

One of the biggest, oldest, and most diverse communities on the web. While it has a homepage displaying the most popular news stories of the day, Reddit is actually compromised of endless "subreddits", each focused around a subject such as Star Wars, Art, Memes, and more.

**FREE**

### LinkedIn: Job Search & News
Network & Find Jobs For You
★★★★☆ 10K

Think of LinkedIn as a social media platform for careers. After creating a profile detailing your career and skills, you're able to search for jobs, and network with similar people.

**FREE**

# Essential productivity apps

## Edit a complex spreadsheet, create a short film and more...

The iPad represents a fully-fledged replacement for the traditional PC or laptop, capable of running multiple apps side-by-side on a single screen. Explore the App Store, and you'll find a plethora of apps focused on productivity and timekeeping. Here are just a few...

### Pages
Documents that stand apart
★★★☆☆ 3.2K

Think of Pages as Microsoft Word, but it's made by Apple and is free for the iPad. Using Pages you can create documents and letters, and even open and edit Word files.

**FREE**

### Keynote
Build stunning presentations
★★★⯪☆ 1.6K

Keynote is Apple's answer to Microsoft's Powerpoint, enabling you to create beautiful presentations and slideshows. There are loads of templates and animations to choose from, so you can quickly create a presentation in minutes that'll wow anyone that sees it.

**FREE**

### Numbers
Create impressive spreadsheets
★★★☆☆ 1.3K

If you need to create spreadsheets on your iPad, then Numbers is the app of choice. It works surprisingly well on a touchscreen, while also being able to open Excel files.

**FREE**

### Grammarly Keyboard
Type with confidence
★★★★☆ 2.3K

Grammarly is a professional editor and spell checker, able to improve your writing and grammar in real-time. It will suggest alternative words, fix broken sentences, and generally help to improve anything you write.

**FREE**

### Microsoft Office
Word, Excel, PowerPoint & More
★★★★⯪ 1.6K

There are individual apps available for the Microsoft Office Suite, but this takes the basics from each and combines them into a single app. You can open and edit Office files, create PDFs, and access your personal cloud storage.

**FREE**

### Focus - Time Management
Pomodoro for Professionals
★★★★☆ 173

If you're a busy person juggling multiple jobs at once, then Focus will help you to perform at your best by splitting your work into multiple sessions. It's basically a timer and reminder merged into one, and focused exclusively around tasks.

**FREE**

### Agenda.
Date-focused note taking
★★★★⯪ 328

Agenda is a combination of a notepad, task manager and journal, but all based around date-focused tasks. If you're someone who attends a lot of meetings and makes important decisions throughout the day, then Agenda will help you track your tasks and thoughts.

**FREE**

### Flow by Moleskine
Sketch. Think. Create.
★★★★☆ 278

This was Apple's iPad app of the year in 2019, and it's easy to see why. Flow takes the legendary Moleskin notebook experience and brings it to life on the iPad, enabling you to create drawings, beautiful art, and notes.

**FREE**

# Essential creativity apps

Create art, edit photos, or layout an app...

The iPad makes for the perfect canvas, able to simulate traditional brushes, clean vector lines, or even 3D models. Here is a selection of apps that will get your creative juices flowing...

### Procreate
Sketch, paint, create.

*Editors' Choice*

An incredible app which enables you to paint or draw using realistic looking brushes. Procreate also supports layers and a powerful undo tool, plus the ability to export a timelapse video of your art coming to life.

**FREE**

### Pixelmator
Photo & Video

*Editors' Choice*

If you need to edit a photo with professional results, or even create a sketch or painting, then Pixelmator is a powerful tool built specifically for the iPad.

**$4.99**

### AutoCAD
DWG Viewer & Editor

★★★★☆ 404

A commercial tool used to design and draft; this iPad iteration enables you to view, edit, and create CAD drawings on the go.

**FREE**

### Adobe Illustrator Draw
Create Vector Art

★★★★½ 6.3K

Although not as powerful as the desktop version of Illustrator, this iPad version still enables you to create amazing illustrations using vector tools. With regular updates over time, it promises to soon become a powerful tool to match its desktop brother.

**FREE**

### uMake - 3D CAD Modeling

Easy 3D Sketch, Draw & Design

★★★★☆ 322

If you've ever wanted to dabble in 3D modeling, then uMake is a great place to start. After creating a 2D sketch, the app can automatically extract a 3D form out of it, enabling you to further tweak and edit as needed.

**FREE**

### Noteshelf

Note-Taking | Handwritten

★★★★☆ 160

If you prefer to sketch notes, rather than write them down, then Noteshelf is the app for you. It enables you to mix hand-drawn images, audio, plus text to create beautiful notes. You can also use the app to annotate PDFs.

**$9.99**

### Adobe Comp

Productivity

★★★★☆ 124

If you need to quickly design an app or website, then Adobe Comp CC is a good place to get started. It enables you to quickly build a wireframe layout, or even add basic shapes, images, and touch hotspots.

**FREE**

### Adobe Fresco  - Draw and Pair

Drawing, painting & sketching

★★★★⯪ 814

Adobe Fresco attempts to replicate the art of painting by simulating paint thickness. You can even smudge the paint with your finger to blend colors and textures. The basic app is free, but for $10 a month, you can unlock more features.

**FREE**

# Best iPad games

Go racing, build a castle, or race your friends...

With a massive touchscreen and powerful GPU underneath its screen, the iPad makes for a genuinely great gaming device. From classic games such as Angry Birds and Minecraft, to full PC classics like Civilization, there's plenty of gaming choice in the App Store. Here are just a few of the best games on offer.

### Asphalt 9: Legends
Epic Arcade Car Racing Game
*Editors' Choice*

Featuring an extensive roster of real-life hypercars from Ferrari, Porsche, Lamborghini and more, this beautiful and fast-paced racing game is a joy to play on the iPad.

**FREE**

### Angry Birds 2
Best arcade action game!
*Editors' Choice*

It's been out for quite some time, but this unique touch-based puzzle game is still one of the best. It tasks the player with destroying towers filled with green pigs. To do this they must use giant slingshots to fire angry birds through the air. Genius.

**FREE**

### Fortnite
Battle Royale & Party Hub
★★★★½ 666K

For a while this took over the competitve gaming world, with fast-paced first-person shooting action. It's still a blast to play, and with regular updates that literately change the virtual world, there's always something new to see and do.

**FREE**

### Minecraft
Create, explore and survive!
*Editors' Choice*

Build literately anything you can imagine, or dig deep into the earth to mine precious resources and craft weapons and armour to survive the hordes of monster which come out at night.

**$6.99**

### Monument Valley 2
A story of beauty and illusion

✦ Editors' Choice ✦

An absolutely beautiful puzzle game which challenges the player to guide a mother and her child through dozens of illusionary puzzles.

**$4.99**

### Sid Meier's Civilization® VI
Build. Conquer. Inspire.

★★★☆☆ 402

The full turn-based strategy game is now available on the iPad, and it works perfectly with touch controls. If you're looking for a time-sink game to fill a lot an afternoon, then this is the perfect choice.

**$19.99**

### Mario Kart Tour
Race around the world!

★★★★★ 89K

It's Mario Kart - but on your iPad! Enjoy competitive racing along dozens of colorful tracks. With support for multiplayer racing, you can also test your skills against up to seven other players too.

**FREE**

### Lara Croft GO
Breathtaking Puzzle Adventure

✦ Editors' Choice ✦

A turn-based adventure game which tasks the player with navigating lush environments and puzzles using simple swipe-to-move controls.

**$4.99**

# Web & Communication

With an iPad in your hand, you're never out of reach from friends and loved ones. Similarly, you have the world's knowledge at your fingertips, thanks to the powerful Safari browser.

Over the next few pages, you'll learn how to browse the web on your iPad, send messages with animated effects, send emails with attachments, make a FaceTime video call, plus much more.

# Use Safari to browse the web

Visit websites, organize tabs, customize your experience, and more...

Browsing the web using Safari on iPad Pro is a wonderful experience. Websites look stunning on the 12.9-inch display, with crisp text and vivid images, and they load in an instant. Thanks to the all-new multitasking capabilities, it's also possible to browse the web while reading your emails, checking out the latest tweets or making a FaceTime call.

This chapter will explain how the Safari app works, how to take advantage of its features and how you can customize the experience to best suit your needs.

You'll find the Safari app already installed on your iPad. To locate it, just unlock your iPad then tap on this icon:

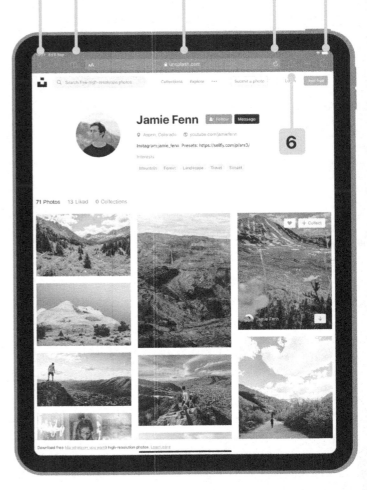

## The basics of using Safari

**1** Use these arrows to go back a page, or forward a page.

**2** Access your favorite websites and bookmarks by tapping this button.

**3** Tap the **search** field to search the web or type a website address.

**4** Tap this curved arrow to refresh the page. **Tap and hold** to view the desktop version of a site.

**5** Tap the **Tabs** button to view all of the tabs open on your iPad.

**6** Tap the **Share** button to send a webpage to another iPad, message a link, email a link, print the page and much more.

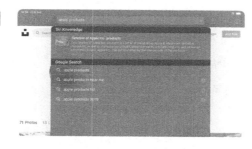

### How to enter a website address

To visit a website, tap on the address field and enter an URL via the on-screen keyboard. Tap the blue **Go** button on the keyboard to visit the site.

### How to search the internet

The address bar in Safari also acts as a search engine, so to search the web for any question or search term, just type your query into the address bar at the top of the screen.

### Search suggestions

As you type into the address bar, notice that Safari offers search suggestions in real-time. Tap on a suggestion or the blue **Go** button on the keyboard to confirm your query.

### Tabs

Think of a tab as a single view of a webpage. You can have as many tabs open on your iPad as you like, but you can only view one at a time.

### Access the Tabs view

To access the tabs view, tap the **tabs** button in the very top-right corner of the screen. It looks like two overlapping squares.

### Open and close Tabs

To open a new tab view, press the **plus** button at the top of the screen. To close a tab, press the small **X** button in it's top-left corner.

### Re-open a closed tab

If you accidentally closed a tab and want to go back to it, press and hold the **tab** button and after a second a pop-up window will appear showing your recently closed tabs.

### Enable Private Browsing

You can browse the web without saving any history, searches, passwords or field entries by enabling Private Browsing mode. To do this, tap the **Tabs** button, then tap the **Private** button. You'll then notice the Safari interface change color from white to dark grey. To disable Private Browsing mode, re-open the **tabs** window then tap the **Private** button again.

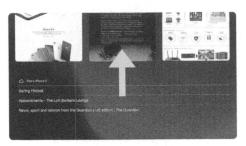

### iCloud tabs

Using iCloud, tabs are automatically synced across all of your Apple devices. To access them, tap the **tabs** button, then push the tab view upwards.

### Customize website settings

While viewing a website, tap the **AA** button next to the address bar to zoom the page, hide the toolbar, request the mobile version of a page, or adjust settings.

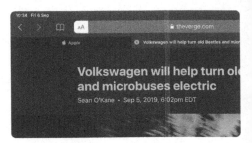

### Remove clutter from web pages

To remove ads and clutter from a webpage, tap the **AA** button, then tap **Show Reader View**.

### Search a web page for text

Looking for a keyword, name, or figure on a web page? By pressing the **Share** button, then tapping **Find on Page**, you can search a web page for anything text-based.

### Block ads and junk from slowing down the web

Using Safari it's possible to install "extensions" which prevent adverts from loading on web pages. To install and active a content blocker, open the App Store and search for *"content blocker"*. Once you've chosen an app install it then go to **Settings > Safari > Content Blockers** and toggle the content blocker app **"on"**.

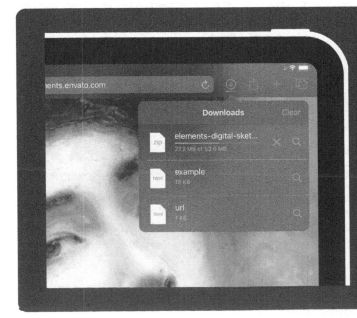

### Download and save files

When you tap to download a file from the internet, a new Downloads button will appear to the right of the address bar. Tap on it to see the progress of a download.

To find your downloaded file/s, open the Files app, then tap on the **Downloads** folder in the sidebar.

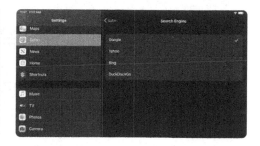

## Clear your web browsing history

If you need to clear your browsing history, go to **Settings > Safari** then tap the **Clear History and Website Data** button.

## Save a webpage as a PDF

To save a website as a PDF on your iPad, take a screenshot by pressing the **power** and **volume down** buttons, tap the thumbnail in the lower corner then choose **Full Page**.

## Change the default search engine

By default, Safari searches the web using results from Google. If you'd rather search using Yahoo!, Bing, or DuckDuckGo, go to **Settings > Safari > Search Engine**.

## Share a page

Sometimes it's helpful to share a website with friends and family. Safari offers a wealth of sharing options, including the ability to email web pages, send an URL via the messages app, and much more.

To access these sharing abilities, tap the **Share** icon at the top of the screen (it looks like a square with an arrow pointing upwards out of it). You'll see the share panel slide up the screen, with icons and shortcuts to each sharing ability. Tap on whichever is most suitable for your needs.

## Quickly type domain addresses

There's no need to manually type .com, .co.uk or .net. Instead, touch and hold the **.com** button on the keyboard to choose from a variety of domain suffixes.

## Go back a page

To go back to the last page, swipe your finger from the very left side of the screen inwards. You can also go forward a page by swiping inwards from the right.

## View two websites at once

While using Safari, bring the Dock up and drag the Safari icon the side of the screen. You'll now open a second window, allowing you to browse two websites at once.

# Check your email

Compose messages, organize your inbox, and more...

Alongside the Messages app, Mail must come close to being on the most used apps on iPad. That's because if you're serious about doing things on the web, like shopping or registering for services, then there's no way to avoid having an email address — it's a basic requirement for so many things.

Thankfully, the Mail app on iPad is easy to use and gets straight to the point. It's designed with a clean, white interface that helps you focus on what's important: your emails. Buttons are colored blue, and basic Multi-Touch gestures enable you to delete messages, flag them and more.

You'll find the Mail app already installed on your iPad Pro. To find it, just unlock your iPad then tap on this icon:

## The basics of using Mail

**1** Use this back arrow to return to the Mailboxes screen, where you can access your Drafts, Sent, Junk, and Trash mailboxes.

**2** Looking for a particular email or recipient? Pull the inbox down then use the **search box** to quickly find it.

**3** Delete an email by tapping the **Trash** icon.

**4** Tap this button to create a new email.

**5** Tap this icon to move an email into another folder.

**6** Reply, forward, flag, or print an email using this arrow button.

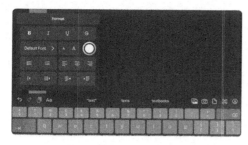

### Quickly format text in an email

If you'd like to bold, italicize or underline a word or sentence, highlight the text then tap on the **option** arrow. Next, tap **BIU** and select the format you wish to use.

### Attach images and videos

To attach an image within an email, tap and hold where you want it to go then tap the **image** button above the keyboard. There's also a camera button for taking a photo on the spot.

### Attach a file from iCloud

To attach a document, PDF, zip file or image saved in iCloud, tap on the **document** button above the keyboard.

## Scan and attach a document

When composing an email, it's possible to scan letters and documents, then attach them directly to a message. What's great is that scans actually look like scanned documents, thanks to some clever post-processing which straightens the image and fixes any white balance issues. To scan a document:

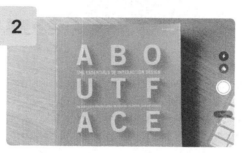

When composting an email, tap the **scan** button above the keyboard.

When the camera view appears, move it over the document you wish to scan and your iPad will automatically recognize it.

Take a photo, then adjust the corners of the scan to match the document.

Tap **Keep Scan** to save the image. You can continue to scan further documents, or tap **Save** to attach the image/s to your email.

The scan will now be attached to your email as an image.

### Format text

While composing an email, tap the Aa button above the keyboard to access a wide range of text editing tools, such as font family, color and layout.

### Delete multiple emails

While viewing your inbox, tap the blue **Edit** text in the top right corner. Next, tap on the messages you'd like to delete, you can select as many as needed. Once you're happy with the selection, tap the **Delete** button in the bottom-right corner.

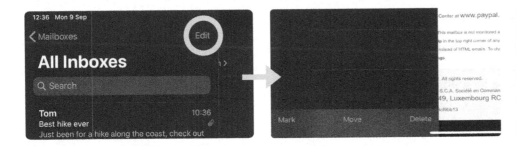

### Move or mark multiple emails

Follow the steps above, but instead of deleting the selected messages select either **Mark** or **Move** at the bottom of the screen. Mark enables you to flag the messages, mark them as unread or move them to the Junk folder. Move enables you to store the emails in a separate folder from the Inbox.

### See contact details

While reading an email, tap on the name of the contact at the top of the message and you'll see their details in full.

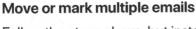

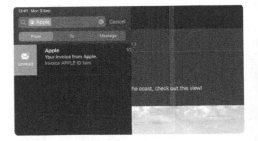

### Get email reply notifications

Waiting for an important reply to an email? You can receive a notification when it arrives by opening the email message, tapping the **arrow** button in the bottom corner, then tap **Notify Me...**

### Save a contact to your device

If you'd like to save an emails contact details to your iPad, then tap on their **name** while reading an email then select either **Create New Contact** or **Add to Existing Contact.**

### Mark an email as Unread

Sometimes it's helpful to mark emails as unread so they can be later re-read or referenced. To do this just swipe the message to the right then choose **Unread**.

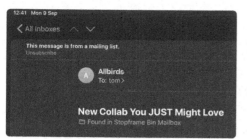

### Automatically unsubscribe

If you receive an unsolicited marketing email and want to quickly unsubscribe, open the message then tap the **Unsubscribe** text at the top of the screen.

### Forward an email

To quickly forward an email to someone else, tap the **arrow** button in the bottom-right corner, then tap **Forward**.

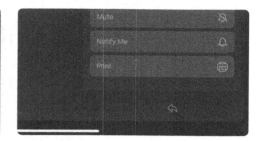

### Print an email

To print an email, tap the **forward arrow** button at the bottom of the screen then tap **Print**. Select a wireless printer then tap **Print**.

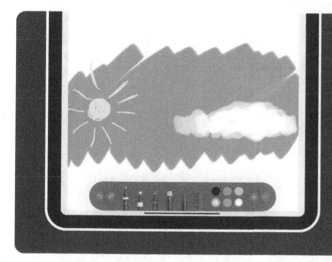

## Attach a drawing

You can attach a drawing to an email by tapping the pencil button above the keyboard. While drawing, you can choose from a variety of tools, such as a pencil, felt tip, marker, or ruler. You can further customize a tool by tapping on it, so tap on the felt tip tool and you'll be able to adjust the line thickness and opacity.

### Delete an email with a swipe

Erasing emails can become a chore, so to speed up the process, simply **swipe your finger right-to-left** across the email message while in the Inbox.

### More email options

After swiping an email from right-to-left, tap the **More** button and you'll see a selection of controls appear. Options include Reply, Forward, Mark, Notify, and Move.

### Save a draft email

If you're composing an email and you're not ready to send it yet, drag the email down to the bottom of the screen. It'll stay there, below the rest of your emails, until you tap on it to continue the draft.

# Chat using Messages

Send messages, photos, emojis, and even animated faces...

You might not think of the iPad as a device for sending messages, but that's exactly what you can do with the Messages app. For those times when your iPhone isn't to hand, it can prove to be a surprisingly fun and useful app, and because your messages are synced across all of your Apple devices, you can start a conversion on your iPad and continue it later on your iPhone.

To find the Messages app on your iPad, just look for the green app icon with a speech bubble:

## The basics of using Messages

**1** Tap the **New Message** button to start a conversation.

**2** Tap on a persons name or image to see more details about them.

**3** Tap the **Camera** button to take a photo on the spot, or tap the **Photos** button to send an image from your library.

**4** Tap and hold the **Microphone** button to send an audio message. Let go when you've finished recording.

**5** Access a variety of characterful emojis by tapping this button.

**6** If you need to move the cursor around, tap and hold on the **spacebar** to turn the keyboard into a trackpad.

# What's an iMessage...

This is a message sent directly from one Apple device to another. iMessages are sent completely free, are automatically encrypted between devices (so no one can read them), can be sent over a Wi-Fi network, and can contain video content, photos, audio, and maps. There's also no character or size limit, so your messages can be as long or as complicated as you like. iMessages always appear as blue bubbles in the chat window, while regular SMS messages appear green.

### How to send a new message

Tap the **New Message** icon in the top-right corner of the Messages inbox. In the **To**: field, begin to type the name of a contact, their email address or a phone number. If the contact already exists on your iPad then you'll see their name appear above the keyboard. You can tap on this entry to automatically fill the To: field, or continue to enter the recipient's details until complete.

### Send a message

Once you've entered a recipients contact details, tap the text entry field just above the keyboard, then type a message. Once you're ready to send, tap the **blue arrow** button (sometimes it's green if the other person doesn't have an iPad or iPhone), above the keyboard and the message will be sent.

### Explore the App Drawer

The app drawer within the Messages app lets you do incredible things like share your travel plans, discover a song using Shazam, send stickers, and more.

To find it, look above the keyboard and you'll find the App Drawer. Tap on an app icon to use it, or tap the **App Store** icon to discover more apps.

### Delete a conversation

There are two ways to remove chat conversations from the Messages app. The simplest is to **swipe right-to-left** across the chat conversation from the home page of the Messages app. Alternatively, tap the **Edit** button at the top of the Messages screen, select the conversation/s that you wish to delete, then tap the **Delete** button.

### See when a message was sent

Here's a great tip that goes unnoticed by most: to see the exact time a message was sent or received, **slide the chat window to the left** using your finger. You'll see the chat bubbles slide to one side and the time each was sent/received appear.

## Create your very own Memoji

Sending a video message of your face is so 2017, because with the new Memoji feature, you can now create your very own 3D avatar, then use it to send fun animated messages to friends and family. Here's how it works:

**1** Open the **Messages** app, then tap on the **Animoji** button. It looks like a monkeys face.

**2** Tap the **+** button to create a custom Memoji. Scroll to the left if you don't see it.

**3** Use the creation tool to create your very own Memoji.

**4** Tap **Done** in the top-right corner to save and use your new Memoji.

Let's take a more detailed look at some of the Memoji options available:

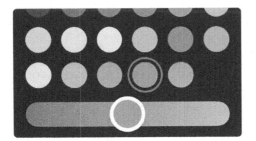

### Skin colors

Memojis start life with yellow skin, but you're given 17 other colors to choose from including green, blue, or purple.

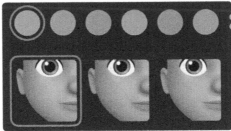

### Freckles, cheeks & beauty spots

While choosing a skin color, you can also choose from three types of freckles, four cheek blushes, and six beauty spot placements.

### Hairstyle

There's a wealth of hairstyles to choose from, and each can be customized with highlights or unique colors.

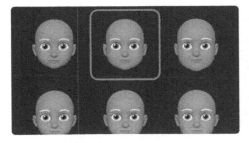

### Head shape

Choose from a selection of head shapes. There are also three different ages to select.

### Eyes, eyelashes and brows

Select from 9 eye shapes, 9 eyelash designs, and 15 types of eyebrow.

### Nose and Lips

Whatever shape nose you have, you'll find the corresponding shape here in the Memoji creator. You can also pick from a range of lip shapes, colors and piercings.

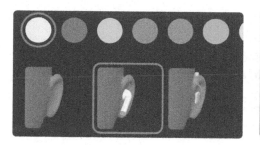

**Ears**

The Memoji creator includes a large selection of ear types to choose from. You can also add earrings and studs – or even a pair of Airpods.

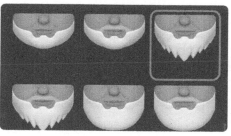

**Facial Hair**

The Memoji creator comes with 3 types of facial hair: moustache, beard, and sideburn. There are dozens to choose from, and of course, they can each be customized using color.

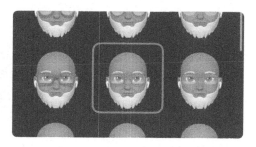

**Eyewear**

Whether you wear glasses or sunglasses, you'll find a large amount of eyewear types to choose from. You can even change the lens color using a secondary control.

## Replace your head with an Memoji or Animoji

If you want to really surprise someone, then sending a photo or video of yourself with your face replaced with an Memoji, is a good way to do that. What's particularly impressive is that the Memoji matches your head movements perfectly. There's even a subtle shadow below to make it look almost realistic. Here's how it works:

**1** Tap the **Camera** icon to the left of the message field.

**2** Tap the **Effects** button in the bottom-left corner.

**3** Tap the **Animoji** button.

**4** Choose a Memoji.

**5** Press the small **X** button to close the Animoji panel.

**6** Pose, then take a photo.

**7** Press the **white** button to send your snap.

## Send an Animoji

Using the Messages app you can create and send animated emojis using your face. Animojis track more than 50 facial movements and can be used to create amazing animated expressions. To create and send an Animoji:

1. When you're viewing or replying to a message, tap the **Animoji** icon. It looks like a monkeys face.

2. You'll immediately see the Animoji come to life on the screen as it mirrors your facial expressions and head movements.

3. To navigate through the different Animojis, slide the panel of faces sideways. To see all of them at once, slide the Animoji panel upwards.

4. Tap the **record** button, and the Animoji will start recording. Say your message out-loud and play around with expressions.

5. After you're done, tap the **record** button to end. You'll see a preview of the recording. To send the Animoji, just tap the blue **Send** button.

## Send an emoji

Emoji's are awesome. Each one is a beautifully designed graphic that represents a word, emotion or object, and by mixing emoji's with words you can really add emotion or humor to a message.

To send an emoji tap the **Emoji** button on the keyboard while composing a message. It's at the bottom of the screen next to the spacebar and microphone. You can swipe left and right to scroll through emoji's or tap the grey icons at the bottom of the screen to jump to an emoji category.

# Add a camera effect or filter to a photo

If you want to add a filter to a photo, a caption, make an annotation, or add a cool effect, then here's how:

**1** Tap the **Camera** icon to the left of the message field.

**2** Take a photo or video.

**3** Tap the **Effects** button in the bottom-left corner.

**4** Use the **Effects**, **Edit**, or **Markup** buttons to add effects to your photo or video.

**5** Press the **white/blue** send button to send the photo or video.

**To add a filter to a photo:**

Tap on the **Effects** button, tap on **Filters**, then tap on a filter to preview it.

**To add text or speech bubbles:**

Tap on the **Effects** button, tap on **Text**, then choose a text style. You'll find 18 types of text effects to choose from. When you've made a selection, you can enter your own text, move the text or re-size it with two fingers.

**To add a shape:**

Tap on the **Effects** button, **Shapes**, then chose from one of the 15 shapes..

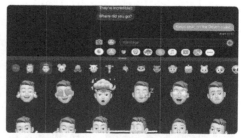

**Assign a profile photo or Animoji avatar**

Assigning a profile photo is a great way to personalize conversations and let people know who they're talking too; and if you don't want to use a photo, then it's possible to assign a custom Animoji instead. To do this tap on the **options** button in the top-left corner, tap **Edit Name and Photo**, then choose a photo or tap an Animoji.

**To send a Memoji sticker:**

Tap on the **Memoji** button to attach a fun sticker to your photo. To add some humor, try resizing a Memoji sticker to replace your own head.

## Automatically turn words into emoji's

So you've composed a message, but you want to liven it up with some fun emoji's. It's surprisingly easy, thanks to a clever feature that automatically scans your message for emoji-related words then lets you replace. Here's how:

**1** Compose a message with some emoji-friendly words (such as "happy", "fireworks", "pizza" etc).

**2** Tap the **emoji** button on the keyboard. Any emoji-friendly words will glow gold.

**3** Tap on the gold words that you'd like to replace and they will automatically swap from text to emoji graphics.

## Send a Digital Touch drawing

With the Messages app you can draw a message and send it with just a few taps of your finger. Here's how it works:

**1** When you're viewing or replying to a message, tap the **Digital Touch** button in the App Store panel. It looks like two fingertips over a heart.

**2** Start to draw on the black panel in the bottom half of the screen. You'll see your drawing come to life.

**3** Once you've finished tap the **blue arrow** icon to send the drawing.

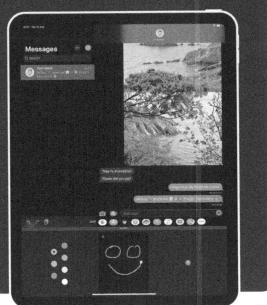

It's not just a drawing you can send, there are five other effects including a heart beat and a fireball:

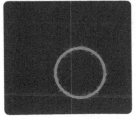

**Taps**

Simply tap anywhere on the black panel and an animated tap will appear.

**Fireball**

Press and hold on the screen with your finger. When you let go a fireball effect will be sent.

**Kiss**

Tap with two fingers and you'll send a kiss message.

**Heartbeat**

Tap and hold on the screen and an animated heartbeat will be sent.

**Broken Heart**

Tap and hold with two fingers then slide downwards to send a broken heart.

# Send a message with an animated effect

If you'd like to emphasize a message with an animated effect then four hidden effects are included within the Messages app: a slam dunk, a loud shout, gentle whisper, or invisible ink – where the recipient must swipe their finger across the message to reveal it. Here's how it works:

**1** Compose your text, then instead of tapping the blue send arrow, **tap and hold** on it.

**2** In the pop-up window, tap one of the four options on the right-side of the screen to see a preview of how it looks.

**3** Once you're happy with an effect, tap the **blue arrow** to send the message.

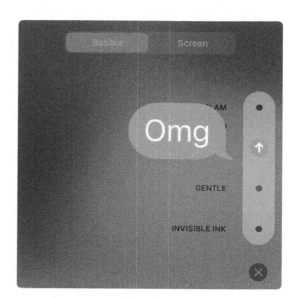

### Add a Tapback sticker

If you want to add a personal touch to a delivered message just **tap and hold** on the message bubble to see six stickers that can be attached and seen by the recipient.

### To see the details of a contact

Tap on their **name** or **image** at the top of the screen then choose **Info**. On the following panel, tap on the **small arrow** at the top of the screen to see the recipients details.

### Share your current location

Meeting a friend somewhere in town? If they're having trouble finding you, tap on their **name** at the top of the screen, choose **Info**, then tap the **Send My Current Location** button.

### Search for people, photos & more

From the home screen of the Messages app, pull the screen down to reveal a search bar. Tap on this and you'll be able find recent contacts, links, photos and search through message content.

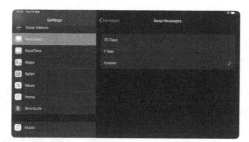

### Automatically delete messages

You can tell Messages to automatically remove chats after either 30 days or 1 year. To activate this feature, go to **Settings > Messages > Keep Messages**.

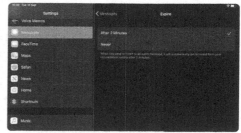

### Keep audio messages

By default, audio messages are automatically deleted after 2 minutes. To keep them forever, go to **Settings > Messages**, then scroll down where you'll see an option for storing audio messages for longer.

# Make a FaceTime video call

Make a free video call to friends and family using FaceTime...

With FaceTime, you can be with friends and family at any time and place. Whether it's a birthday, anniversary, meeting or just a chat, FaceTime lets you be a part of the moment with crystal clear video and audio.

FaceTime works over both Wi-Fi or a cellular connection, and enables you to call another iPad, iPhone, iPod touch, or a Mac. It works like a phone call, but it's free, supports video, and you can even add realtime filters effects.

You'll find the FaceTime app already installed on your iPad. To find it, just tap on this icon:

## The basics of using FaceTime

1  You can move the preview image of yourself around the screen by dragging it with your finger.

3  End the call using this button.

5  Flip your camera around using this button to show what's behind your iPad.

2  Drag the **Effects** panel upwards to access additional controls.

4  Tap the **Effects** button to apply a wide range of filters, shapes, and video effects.

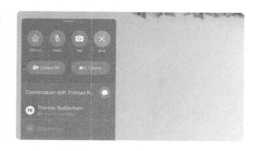

### Make a FaceTime call

Open the FaceTime app and sign in if you haven't used it before. You'll see your contacts listed down the middle of the screen. Tap a contact to automatically begin calling them.

### Access additional controls

During a FaceTime call, drag the **lower panel upwards** to access additional controls, including the ability to disable your camera, or begin a chat conversation.

### Delete your history

From the main FaceTime screen, tap the **Edit** button in the top-left corner, select any conversations you would like to clear, then tap **Delete**.

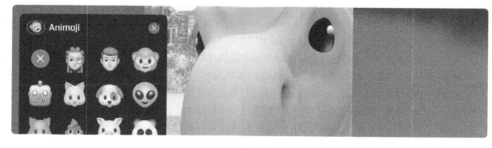

### Add stickers and filters

While making a FaceTime call, tap the **Effects** button in the lower panel to explore a wide range of video effects.

### Replace your face with a Memoji

During the FaceTime call, tap the **Effects** button in the bottom-left corner. Tap on the **Animoji** icon (it looks like a monkey), then select an existing avatar, or custom-made Memoji.

## Make a regular phone call

Yes, you can use your iPad Pro as a giant telephone. It works by routing the call through your iPhone in the background without you knowing. To do this:

1. Select a contact using the list on the left-side of the screen, or tap the **plus** button, then type a contacts name.

2. You can also type a phone number, then tap the blue plus button.

3. Tap the **Audio** button. Your iPad will then dial the number and make the call through your iPad.

4. t

# Camera and Photos

The iPad Pro is probably one of the best cameras you own. Not because it has the best image quality or the highest megapixels, but because it's built into the device which you use everyday, so it's ready to capture a special moment, then share it with everyone you know. It's also really clever. Using the iPad it's possible to take Burst Mode photos, capture slow-motion videos, or simply take a great picture, then tweak it with some incredibly powerful editing tools.

That's what this chapter is all about. You'll get to know the Camera app in all its glory, then discover how to edit and share your photos with friends and family. Before you know it, you'll be a budding photographer with a library of stunning images.

# Take amazing photos

## Get to know the camera app and all of its features...

The iPad might not be the first choice of camera for many, but that hasn't stopped millions from capturing magical moments and memories on the spot. iPad Pro continues that tradition, with an 12-megapixel camera that's capable of taking beautiful photos, can capture 4k video, and even film in slow motion. Additionally, the front-facing FaceTime camera is great for making video calls, taking a fun selfie, or recording your own Memoji.

Helping you to capture these moments is the Camera app. It's simple and intuitive to use, yet offers so many possibilities. To find the Camera app, just look for this icon:

## The basics of using the Camera app

**1** Tap the **1X** button to zoom out and use the ultra-wide lens. You can also tap and hold on this button to manually set a zoom level.

**2** Toggle Live Photo mode on or off by using this button.

**3** Tap this button to set a timer.

**4** Enable / disable the flash on the back of your iPad.

**5** Swap between the front or back facing cameras.

**6** Take a photo, or tap and hold to capture a Burst Mode photo.

**7** Jump to your most recently taking photo by tapping this thumbnail image.

**8** You can swap between camera modes by swiping or tapping the shortcut buttons here.

### Take a photo from the lock screen

The quickest way to open the Camera app is via the lock screen of your iPad. To do this, just **swipe the Lock Screen from right-to-left** and the Camera viewfinder will appear.

### Live Photos

Whenever you take a photo, your iPad captures a few frames before and after the shot. To view this back, just **press and hold** on the image when viewing it in the Photos app.

### Turn Live Photos off

If you don't need (or like) the Live Photo feature, then you can disable it by tapping the yellow **Live Photo** icon on the right-side of the screen.

### Capture using the volume buttons

It's possible to take a photo by pressing the **volume up or down** buttons on the side of your iPad. This is especially useful for taking selfies with your arm outstretched.

### Zoom even further

You can zoom up to 5x digitally by using the slider on the left side of the screen. You can also pinch your fingers on the viewfinder to zoom in or out.

### Camera focus

The camera will automatically focus onto a prominent object or area of light, but if you need to manually focus the camera, just tap on the area or subject you wish to focus on.

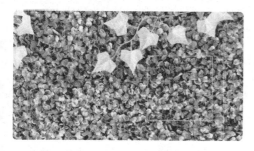

### Lock the focus and aperture

To lock the focus and aperture levels, **tap and hold** on a subject or area. After a second or two a flashing yellow box beneath your finger will indicate that the camera focus has been locked.

### Swap camera modes

The Camera app has multiple modes, including Photo, Portrait, Video, Slow-Mo, Square and Pano. To quickly jump between them, swipe your finger up or down across the shortcut buttons on the right-side of the screen.

### Turn the flash on and off

To toggle the flash off, tap the **lightning** button on the right-side of the screen. You'll see options for activating the flash automatically, turning it on or off.

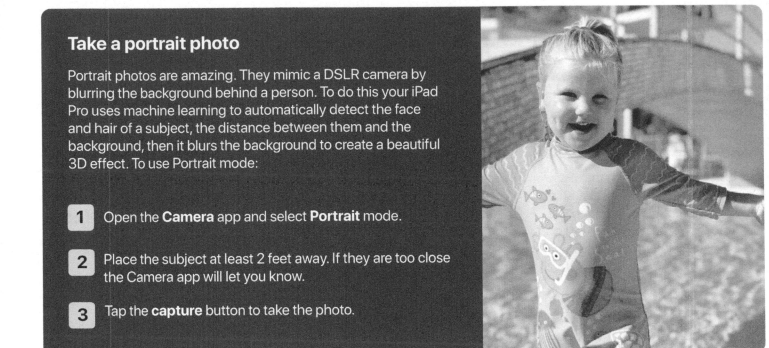

## Take a portrait photo

Portrait photos are amazing. They mimic a DSLR camera by blurring the background behind a person. To do this your iPad Pro uses machine learning to automatically detect the face and hair of a subject, the distance between them and the background, then it blurs the background to create a beautiful 3D effect. To use Portrait mode:

**1** Open the **Camera** app and select **Portrait** mode.

**2** Place the subject at least 2 feet away. If they are too close the Camera app will let you know.

**3** Tap the **capture** button to take the photo.

## Use Portrait Lighting to take amazing selfies

By using Portrait Lighting mode you can simulate a number of professional photographer effects and tools, such as a gold bounce card, to create even more beautiful looking photos. There are six effects to choose from:

| **Natural Light** | **Studio Light** | **Contour Light** | **Stage Light** | **Stage Light Mono** | **High-Key Mono** |
|---|---|---|---|---|---|
| Your subject's face in sharp focus against a blurred background. | A clean look with your subject's face brightly lit. | Adds subtle shadows and highlights to the subject's face. | Your subject's face is spotlit against a deep black background. | Like Stage Light, but in black and white. | Adds a beautiful monochromatic effect. |

To enable Portrait Lighting mode, open the **Camera** app and select **Portrait**. You'll see five buttons appear towards the bottom of the screen: Natural Light, Studio Light, Contour Light, Stage Light and Stage Light Mono. Select an effect by swiping through the options. Watch the screen to see the effect apply to your face in real-time. Press the **capture** button to take a photo.

You can choose another effect, even after the photo has been saved, by tapping the **Edit** button within the Photos app.

### Disable the Portrait mode effect

To disable the Portrait effect in a photo, open the image, tap **Edit**, then tap the yellow **Portrait** button at the top of the photo.

### Shoot a video

Capturing video is easy, just swipe your finger across the camera viewfinder until the **VIDEO** is centered, then tap the **red** button.

### Enable 4K video recording

To enable 4K video recording, open the **Settings** app, tap **Camera**, then select **Record Video**. On the following panel you'll be able to enable video recording at 4K.

### Slow motion video

One of the most fun camera features included with iPad is the ability to shoot video in slow motion at 240 frames per second. It's great for capturing fast-moving objects.

### Film in slo-mo

While in the Camera app, swipe the text at the bottom of the screen until **SLO-MO** is centered. Next, tap the red record button to start filming your slow motion video

### Edit the playback speed of a slow-mo video

To edit the slow-motion parts of a video, open the video in the **Photos** app, then tap the **Edit** button.

You'll notice a timeline at the bottom of the screen that's broken up by thin white lines. In the center the lines are spaced further apart. This is the part of the clip which plays back in slow motion.

You can lengthen or shorten this slow motion part of the clip by dragging the white handles, then preview the clip by tapping the play button.

## Burst mode

Action photos have typically been hard to capture on tablet devices. Whether it's someone jumping mid-air, a vehicle racing past, or a friend performing acrobatic moves, these fast-paced photos usually come out blurry or mistimed.

To make things easier, the Camera app on iPad comes with a feature called Burst Mode. It works by taking 10 photos every second, then saves them as a collection within the Photos app. Once the collection has been saved, your iPad automatically scans the images, then picks what it thinks is the best one. It does this by analyzing the brightness and sharpness, and by looking for faces within the image. This is then saved as a Favorite image. If it doesn't pick the right image, or if you want to save multiple snaps from a collection, then you can of course, manually pick your own favorite.

**Capture a burst mode photo**

When you're ready to take a burst mode photo, **tap and hold** the **camera** button. Let go when you've captured the moment.

**Burst mode stacks**

The burst mode images will now be saved as a stack within the Photos app. To see them, tap the **thumbnail** image in the bottom corner of the Camera app. You can also open the **Photos** app to see your saved photo stack.

## Select a burst mode favorite

Open the stack of photos. To select a favorite, tap the **Favorites...** button at the bottom of the screen. A selection of thumbnails will appear. Scroll through them using your finger and tap on your favorite image. If you want to keep multiple images just tap on them, each will be checked with a blue tick.

Tap the **Done** button to confirm your changes. A slide-up panel will ask if you'd like to only keep your favorite/s or keep everything. Tap whichever is relevant to your needs.

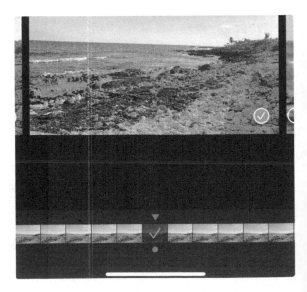

## How to use the Camera timer

To enable the timer, open the **Camera** app and look for a **timer** icon just above the photo button. Tap it and you'll see three text options appear: **Off**, **3s** and **10s**. These correspond to the timer settings, so off is the standard setting, 3s gives you three seconds to pose, and 10s gives you 10 seconds to prepare yourself. Tap whichever you need, then tap the **Camera** button to snap a photo. You'll see a countdown appear on-screen and the camera flash will also emit a brief light for each passing second. After the countdown has ended your iPad will quickly capture 10 photos in a second. This stack of photos will be saved in the Photos app.

To pick a favorite, open the stack and tap the blue **Select...** text. Next, swipe through the images then tap the image (or images) you wish to save. Once you're happy with the selection, tap the **Done** button.

## Capture time-lapse video

Have you ever wanted to capture a sun set, the changing tides, or the movement of clouds? Using the Camera app you can do this with the time-lapse feature. It works by capturing multiple photos, instead of video, over a period of time.

To capture a time-lapse video, open the **Camera** app, then select **TIME-LAPSE**. Next, place your iPad in a suitable location. Make sure it's steady – any movements over time will ruin the time-lapse effect. When you're ready, tap the **red record** button. Leave your iPad for a few moments or minutes - the longer the better as you'll capture more footage - then tap the red record button again to end the time-lapse.

## Panoramic photos

Have you ever wanted to capture an incredibly beautiful vista? By using the PANO mode you can do just this by taking a super-wide, 180-degree photo.

PANO mode works by taking one very wide continuous photo. As you rotate on the spot, the camera captures the image as it appears on the right side of the lens. If there's any movement in front of you (such as people walking by), then you might see a few visual errors, but for vistas and still scenes the PANO mode works wonders.

## Capture a panoramic shot

Begin by opening the **Camera** app, then select **PANO**. You'll see a thumbnail in the center of the screen with a white arrow pointing right. Tap the **Camera** button at the bottom of the screen to start capturing a panoramic shot. Slowly pan your device to the right. Keep a steady hand — if you wobble too much black bars will appear at the top and bottom of the photo. When you've captured the scene, tap the **Camera** button again to end the shot.

## Enable the camera grid

Taking level photos can be tricky when only using the preview window, so to help line up horizons, try enabling the camera grid. To do this, go to **Settings > Camera**, then toggle the **Grid** button on.

Next, go back to the Camera app and you'll see a 3x3 grid above the preview window.

## Preserve Camera Settings

Every time you close the Camera app, then re-open it, it defaults back to the Camera mode; no matter what you were doing before. If you want to reuse a specific mode, such as the video camera, swiping back to it over and over again can be a real pain. Thankfully, there's an easy way to preserve the camera mode you were using last. Just go to **Settings > Camera > Preserve Settings** and toggle **Camera Mode** on.

# View and edit your Photos

Learn how to view, organize, and edit your photos...

The Photos app is a portal to your memories. Stored within its colorful icon are hundreds, if not thousands of treasured photos and videos. Photos of yapping dogs, family members, stunning landscapes, unflattering selfies, and treasured holidays. This is one of those apps that you're going to be opening on a day-to-day basis, so keep it somewhere prominent on the Home screen where you can quickly tap it.

Open the app, and you'll discover a clean, tidy interface that appears to be basic and easy to use. In many ways it is, but dig a little deeper, and you'll find one of the most productive and in-depth apps available for the iPad. With just one fingertip it's possible to edit photos, create albums, move and delete images, view memories, and much more.

To find the Photos app, look for the colorful flower icon:

## The basics of using the Photos app

**1** Tap on a day, month or year to zoom into that date, or alternatively keep tapping inwards.

**2** Tap on the small plus/minus button to zoom in and out. You can also pinch to zoom into your photos.

**3** Tap the **Photos** button to come back to this view, where you can see an overview of all your snaps.

**4** Tap on **For You** to see a memory of a day trip, a birthday, a family gathering, or even a "Best of 2019" album.

**5** Tap **Albums** to view categories of photos, videos, people, slow-mo videos, and more.

**6** Select **Search** to look for nearly anything in a photo, including both people and objects.

## All Photos

When viewing All Photos, you'll see a nearly endless grid of photos scrolling upwards and off the screen. You can scroll through them and tap on an image to see it bigger, or you can pinch to zoom in or out to see your photos spread over a wider range of time.

## Days

Tap on the Days button and you'll see a beautiful grid of images representing a single day. The Photos app intelligently organizes your images, hiding duplicates while selecting a highlighted image or video.

## Months

The Months view organizes the most meaningful events into groups, then displays them as individual cards in a scrollable panel. The app tries to intelligently select the best photo or video to remind you of what the event was about. Think of it as a greatest hit library of your memories.

## Years

Years gives you a high-level overview of your photo library, but what makes this view really special is it's dynamic and based on context. So open the Years view on your birthday and you'll see photos from your birthday celebrations going back as far as your photo library extends.

## Photos

Tap on the **Photos** button at the bottom of the screen and you'll see every photo ever taken using your iPad. You can zoom out to see more images by tapping the blue arrow in the top-left corner. Tap it again and it'll zoom even further out...

The Photos app instantly reads the location and time data within each photo and uses them to sort the images. So if you're on holiday in San Francisco and take 10 photos by the Golden Gate Bridge, these will appear as a moment in the Photos app, titled *"Bay Bridge, San Francisco CA"*.

## For You

Next to the Photos button at the bottom of the screen is **For You**. This is one of the most powerful features of the Photos app. It works by organizing your images into events and albums, then presents these events in chronological order for you to enjoy.

Every day a new set of moments, people, and categories will appear. Tap on one and you'll see more details about the moment, including the location and date.

## Share an event

Whenever the For You section displays a new moment, it will offer the ability to share the corresponding photos with whoever is included in the moment, so if you go hiking with a buddy, the Photos app will let you share all the images with them in just a few steps. Here's how:

1. Select one of the moments in the **Sharing Suggestions** field.
2. If someone you know appears in the photos, tap **Next.**
3. On the following panel, tap **Share in Messages**.
4. You can also add additional people from your contacts list by tapping **+ Add People**.

## Watch a video of an event

Whenever the Photos app suggests a moment, it will also offer the ability to watch it back as a video. To do this:

1. Open the **Photos** app, tap **For You**, then choose a moment which appears.
2. Tap the small blue **options** button in the top-right corner.
3. Select **Play Movie** from the pop-up field.

## Edit a memory video

1. Begin playing the video, then pause it.
2. Notice the **options** above the scrub bar. They enable you to choose a theme and adjust the overall length of the video.
3. Tap on a theme (such as **Gentle** or **Happy**), then press **play** to see the changes made.
4. Similarly, tap on a new duration then press **play** to see the changes.
5. To save the video, tap the **Share** button in the bottom left corner then choose **Save Video.**

# Search through your photos

The Photos app is incredibly intelligent. Using complex visual algorithms it can recognize objects, faces and places, then automatically organize groups of images into albums for you to enjoy. This clever form of visual recognition has another benefit: intelligent searching. You can access this search feature at any time by tapping the **Search** button at the bottom of the screen.

Search for "*California*" and you'll see all your photos of California. Search for "*Trees*" and you'll see (you guessed it) images of trees. You can be even more specific. So search for "*Trees in California*" and the Photos app will automatically show photos of trees within California. You can try other queries such as "*Tom eating pizza*", or "*Sarah riding a horse*" and the app will instantly present you with the correct results.

**People and Places**

After scanning every photo in your library to look for photos of locations and faces, the Photos app collates them into the **People and Places** section of the Photos app.

**Find People and Places**

To see these images just open the Photos app and go to **Albums > People & Places**.

**Check out the places view**

Tap on the **Places** thumbnail, and you'll see a map view with all of your photos placed in the correct location.

**Watch a video of someone**

To watch a video of someone in the People album, select them then tap the **play** button near the top of the screen.

**Add a name to a person**

To add a name to someone in the People album, tap the **+ Add Name** field at the top of the screen.

**Add someone to Favorites**

If you like to regularly see the photos of a family member or friend, tap the small **heart** icon in the bottom corner of their thumbnail image.

View and edit your Photos

## How to share a photo or video

Open an image, then tap the **Share** icon in the top-right corner of the screen – it looks like a blue box with an arrow pointing upwards.

## Select multiple images

To select multiple photos at once, make sure you're viewing a collection of images then tap the blue **Select** button in the top-right corner of the screen.

## How to delete a photo

While viewing an image tap the blue **Trash** icon in the top-right corner of the screen.

## The basic controls of editing a photo

Want to improve the look of a photo you've taken on your iPad? Begin by selecting an image in the Photos app, then tap the **Edit** button in the top-right corner. You'll see the screen darken, and a number of editing tools appear. Here's a quick overview of each:

**1** Cancel any edits by tapping here.

**2** Pinch to zoom on an image while editing to get a closer look.

**3** Tap the **ellipse** button to add markup to an image.

**4** Tap the **Live Photo** button to disable the live effect, choose a new still, or to mute the Live Photo.

**5** Tap the **Tools** button to access the various editing tools.

**6** Choose from a variety of photo filters.

**7** Crop and rotate an image by tapping this button.

**8** Use the editing tools here to adjust an image.

### Adjustment tools

The second icon on the right-side of the screen enables you to adjust the appearance of an image. When you tap this button, the auto-correct tool is initially selected. Tap this tool to automatically improve the look of an image.

### Fine tune an image

Scroll through the buttons on the right-side of the screen. You'll see tools for adjusting a photos exposure, brilliance, highlights, shadows, contrast, brightness, black point, saturation, vibrance, warmth, tint, sharpness, definition, noise and vignette. Select a tool then use the vertical slider to make fine adjustments. By experimenting with each tool, you'll discover your own favorite settings and adjustments.

### Disable an adjustment tool

To disable and reset an adjustment tool, simply tap on its button. You'll see the button go grey and any adjustments will reset.

### Add a vignette

Scroll all the way to the left and you'll find the Vignette tool. Drag the slider to the left to add a white vignette effect, and to the right to add a dark vignette.

### Compare changes to a photo

If you'd like to compare your changes with the original photo at any time, tap and hold your finger on the thumbnail image above the editing controls.

### Add a filter

The middle icon at the bottom of the screen enables you to add a photo filter to your image. You'll find eight to choose from, each with its own unique appearance.

### Crop an image

Tap the **Crop** icon, then either drag the edges of the image to crop it, or tap the small **ratio** button in the top-right corner to choose from a range of image ratio sizes.

### Rotate or tilt a photo

While cropping a photo you can also rotate or tilt it. To rotate an image, just drag the horizontal slider below the image. To tilt an image, tap one of the two tilt buttons then drag the same horizontal slider.

## Bring a flat image to life

Photos taken using the iPad usually look amazing, but on occasion can look a little flat or overblown due to the small lens and sensor. Thankfully, the Photos app makes it easy to turn flat images into colorful, expressive shots. Here's how it's done:

**1** **Start by editing a photo**
Select an image using the Photos app, then tap the **Edit** button in the top-right corner.

**2** **Adjust the brilliance**
Scroll through the editing tools until **Brilliance** is selected. Now, pull the slider down using your finger and watch as colors and depth are revealed.

**3** **Adjust the highlights**
Scroll through the editing tools again and choose **Highlights**, then drag the slider up and watch how as even more colors appear.

**4** **Edit the Shadows**
Drag the slider along by one tool to select **Shadows**, then drag the slider down by a small amount. You'll see darker areas of the image become brighter and more colorful.

**5** **Color Adjustments**
Next, select the **Saturation** tool, then drag the slider down to subtlety boost the colors of the photo.

**6** **Further adjustments**
Other tools you can experiment with include contrast, warmth and tint. Feel free to experiment, with time you'll discover which tools work best with various scenarios and lighting conditions, and soon you'll be able to improve a photo in just a few seconds.

*Before and after making adjustments to an image.*

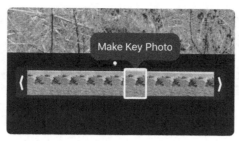

### Edit Live Photos

Live Photos are amazing. They're like the magical moving photos you might have seen in the Harry Potter movies, but they work with your photos. It's also possible to trim the video snippets before or after the photo, select a new keyframe, disable the audio or even change the visual effect animation of the Live photo. Read on to find out how...

### Select a new key frame

If you've taken an action shot and noticed that the exact moment you wanted to capture is in the moving segment of the Live Photo, then you can easily edit the photo and select the exact frame as your key photo. To do this open the photo, tap the **Edit** button, tap the **Live Photo** button, then use the timeline scrubber to choose the new key frame. Once you've found it, tap **Make Key Photo**.

### Trim a Live Photo

Sometimes you might want to trim a part of the Live Photo effect. For example, maybe you suddenly moved the camera at the very last second. Whatever the reason, it's easy to trim the beginning or end.

To get started, select the photo, tap the **Edit** button, then tap the **Live Photo** button. Next, use the handles on either side of the timeline scrubber to fine-tune the start or endpoints.

## Change the animation effect of your Live Photo

The photos app includes some amazing Live Photo effects that can be applied to your image. To apply one, simply open the Live Photo you wish to edit then slide the screen upwards with your finger. You'll see the Effects panel appear beneath. Just tap on the effect of choice to preview and use it.

**Live**
The standard Live Photo effect. To watch it playback, just press firmly on the photo.

**Loop**
This effect turns your Live Photo into a never-ending video loop. If you've ever seen GIF images on the web you'll know how this looks. It works best when the camera is perfectly still, or when there is little movement in the Live Photo.

**Bounce**
Bounce works in a similar way to the Loop effect, except instead of starting the Live Photo again, it plays in reverse once it reaches the end of the clip.

**Long Exposure**
This effect works by combining all the frames of your Live Photo into one image. For the best effect, hold your iPad while taking a photo. Water looks ethereal and misty when viewed through the Long Exposure effect, while moving traffic blurs and streaks across the image.

## Turn off the Live Photo sound

If you don't want to hear the background noise of a Live Photo then select the image, tap the **Edit** button, select the **Live Photo** tool, then tap the yellow **sound** button in the upper-left corner to mute (or unmute) the audio.

## Hide photos

If you'd like to hide a photo from the Photos, Memories and Shared albums, open the photo, tap the **Share** button, scroll down then tap **Hide**. Note that the photo will be copied to a new Hidden album where you can un-hide it if necessary.

## Trim and edit videos

Open a video, tap the **Edit** button and you'll find the same image editing tools, which means you can adjust the light and color of a video, rotate it and even add filters.

You can also trim the beginning and end of a video to adjust its timing and length. To do this tap **Edit** then make a note of the timeline which appears just above the editing tools. By dragging the handles on each side of the timeline you can adjust the start and end points of the video.

## Create an album

If you'd like to organize your photos and videos into albums then tap the **Albums** button at the bottom of the screen. If you've taken or synced any photos then you'll likely see a number of albums already present, including Videos, Burst Mode photos and Slo-mos.

To add an additional album, just tap the blue **plus** icon at the top of the screen. A pop-up window will appear asking for an album title. Enter one using the on-screen keyboard, then tap the **Save** button.

You'll then see a window appear which contains all the available photos on your device. Tap on as many images as you'd like, then tap the **Done** button at the top of the screen. These images will now be added to your new album.

### Rename an album

While viewing the main Albums screen tap the **See All** button in the top-right corner, then on the next screen tap the **Edit** button. You can now re-name albums by tapping on their name. Existing albums such as Recently Added and Recently Deleted can't be re-named, but any albums added by yourself can. Tap on the title of the album and the keyboard will slide up the screen.

### Move an image from one album to another

To move an image from one album to another, select an image then tap the **Share** button. In the pop-up panel, choose **Add to Album**, then select the album you wish to copy the image too.

### Delete an album

It's easy to delete albums from your iPad. While viewing the main Albums screen tap the **See All** button in the top-right corner, then on the next screen tap the **Edit** button. Small red buttons will appear alongside any albums you've created. Tap any of these and the album will be deleted from your iPad.

## Create a shared album

By using shared albums, it's possible to share a selection of images with your friends and family. They can leave comments, like photos, and save them to their device. Here's how it works:

**1** Tap the **Albums** button at the bottom of the screen.

**2** Tap the **plus** icon in the top-left corner, then choose **New Shared Album**.

**3** In the pop-up window, give the album a name (such as "*Holiday*"), then tap the **Next** button.

**4** On the following panel select contacts to share the album with. You can tap their name to enter a contact, or tap the **plus** icon to select people from your contacts book.

**5** Once you've added a bunch of friends or family, tap the **Create** button. The blank album will appear on-screen, to add photos and videos just tap the blue text that reads **Add Photos or Videos**.

# Music and Video

With an Apple Music subscription, you have the world's music at your fingertips, whenever and wherever you are. With Apple Music you can stream the latest tracks, download entire albums to your iPad, and even watch exclusive TV shows; and even if you're not a subscriber, then it's still possible to purchase and download music from the iTunes Store.

# Listen to Music

## Listen to your favorite tracks and albums on Apple Music...

The Music app has always been the best way to listen to music on iPad. It has a beautiful interface, access to millions of tracks via Apple Music, exclusive TV shows, curated playlists, videos, top charts, and Beats 1 Radio.

There's a limitless source of music available in Apple Music, but it comes at a price: to access the full service you'll need to pay a monthly subscription. It's priced slightly differently for each country but roughly works out about the same as a large takeaway pizza. For anyone who listens to the latest charts, streams music on a daily basis or has a wide variety of music tastes, it's definitely worth the asking price. For everyone else, Apple Music still offers Beats 1 Radio, the ability to follow artists and preview music.

To find the Music app on your iPad, just look for this icon:

## The basics of using Music

**1** Tap this button to jump between playlists, artists, albums, films, or downloaded music.

**2** Tap on an album to explore it, or tap and hold to delete it, share it, or Love/Dislike it.

**3** Tap **Library** to access all the music, playlists, and albums saved on your iPad.

**4** Tap **For You** to see playlists created by Apple which suit your tastes, your listening history, what friends are listening too, and new releases.

**5** Tap **Browse** and you'll find the latest tracks, top charts, music videos, and TV shows exclusive to Apple Music.

**6** Tap **Radio** to discover a wide range of radio stations for every taste.

**7** Tap **Search** to find songs, albums, artists, or lyrics, either saved on your iPad or on Apple Music.

**8** Tap on this control panel when a song is playing to access controls, see lyrics, and the rest of the album.

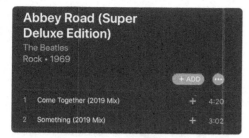

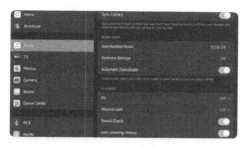

### Add music to your Library

If there's a track or album that you'd like to save to your Library, tap the **+Add** button at the top of the screen.

### Automatically download music

To automatically download music to your iPad whenever you add a new album or track, open the **Settings** app, tap **Music** then toggle **Automatic Downloads** on.

### Browse your offline music

If you don't have an internet connection and need to play music that's saved to your iPad, tap on **Library** then choose **Downloaded Music**.

## View music lyrics in realtime

Have you ever struggled to understand the lyrics of a song as it plays in the background? With iOS 13 you can now get fullscreen lyrics for all your favorite songs, and they update in realtime so you can follow along with the song. Think of it as your own karaoke machine. Here's how it works:

When listening to a song, tap on the small lyrics button in the bottom-left corner of the playback area. It looks like a small speech bubble. You'll then see a fullscreen lyrics view take over. If you don't see the **lyrics** button, just make sure you're looking at the music playback window. You can get to it at any moment by opening the Music app then tapping on the small album artwork thumbnail at the bottom of the screen.

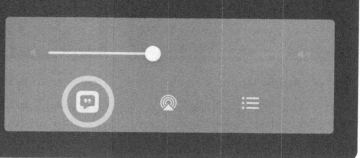

### Shuffle music

If you're bored of an album track order, tap **Shuffle** and you'll never know what song is coming up next.

### Create a Playlist

To create a new playlist of your own, tap **Library**, select **Playlists**, then tap **New** in the top-right corner.

### Add music to an existing playlist

If you'd like to add a track to an existing playlist, tap and hold on the track then choose **Add to a Playlist**. This also works with albums too.

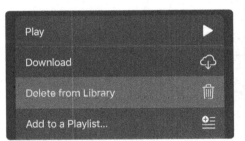

### Delete a track or album

Fed up with a song or album? Just tap and hold on the track name or album artwork, then tap **Delete from Library** in the Share sheet.

### Like music to improve your recommendations list

Whenever you hear a great track or album, tap the **options** button in the corner of the screen (it looks like three dots) then tap the **Love** button. This tells Apple Music what genre of music you like. Keep doing this and over time the For You playlists and recommendations will get more and more accurate to your tastes in music.

### Turn off Apple Music

If you'd like to turn off Apple Music and only see music purchased from the iTunes Store or synced to your device, go to **Settings > Music**, then un-toggle **Show Apple Music**.

### Check out the latest music videos

To browse the latest music videos, open the Music app, tap **Browse**, scroll down then tap **Music Videos**. Tap on a video to watch it, then hold your iPad horizontally to see it full screen.

### See the top charts

What to see what's number one in the charts? Open the **Music** app, tap **Browse**, then tap **Top Charts**.

# Share your music

When you open the Music app for the first time, you'll be asked if you would like to share your music with friends and family. You can tap **Get Started** to set this feature up straight away, or if you'd like to do it later just tap the **For You** button, tap your **user icon** in the top-right corner, then tap the **Edit** button below your name. Here's how it works:

**1** Start by choosing a profile photo and user name.

**2** Tap **Next**, then decide if anyone can follow you, or just those you approve.

**3** Choose if you would like to show your custom playlists within your profile or in search on Apple Music.

**4** Invite your friends to follow you on Apple Music. You can also connect to Facebook to add friends not in your contact book.

**5** Tap **Next** and choose whether you would like to receive notifications when your friends start following you, when they add new playlists, or when there's a new release or mix by one of your favorite artists.

**6** Tap **Done** and you're ready to go.

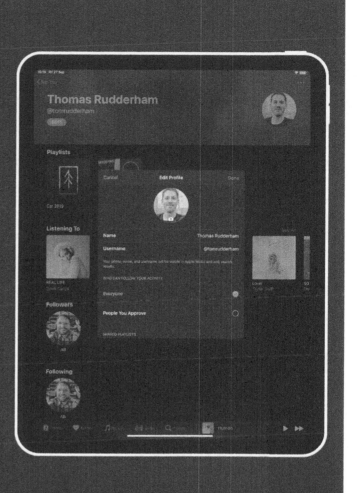

# Watch TV & Movies

Never miss an episode of your favorite show with this helpful app...

With so many sources of video content these days, it has become difficult to keep track of the latest episodes of your favorite TV shows. Thankfully, the Apple TV app for iPad makes it a little bit easier, by collating many of the latest releases into one app. It also houses any TV shows or movies which you've purchased on iTunes, and remembers where you last left off.

To find the Apple TV app on your iPad, just search for it using Spotlight, or look for this icon:

## The basics of using Apple TV

**1** Tap on your profile photo to manage subscriptions, redeem a Gift Card, or sign out.

**2** Quickly jump between movies, TV, or kids shows with these helpful shortcuts.

**3** If you're looking for inspiration, tap **Watch Now** to find suggested TV shows and movies.

**4** You'll find all of your purchases in the **Library** section of the app, split into TV Shows and Movies.

**5** It's pretty obvious, but by tapping **Search** you can look for movies, TV shows, or cast and crew.

### Watch HDR movies on your iPad

If you've purchased any movies with support for HDR playback, tap on **Library,** then scroll down to see a list of HDR-compatible films.

### Find the top rentals

From the **Watch Now** area, scroll down until you find the More to Explore panel. Scroll to the left and you'll find a shortcut to the most popular movie rentals.

### See what's available on Apple TV+

Apple TV+ promises to be a serious competitor to Netflix and Amazon Prime. You can see what's available and coming soon by tapping **Watch Now** then scrolling down.

### Toggle audio sources or subtitles

While watching a video, tap the **speech** icon next to the playback timer to toggle different audio sources or subtitles.

### Access movie special features

To access special features or scene shortcuts, watch a movie in landscape mode. You'll see buttons for special features appear along the bottom of the screen.

### Watch on your Apple TV

If you want to watch a video on your TV, tap the **Apple TV** icon in the bottom-right corner while a video is playing, then choose your Apple TV.

### Download a film to your iPad

If you want to save a purchased film to your iPad, tap on its **artwork**, then tap the **iCloud** button.

### Find out more about cast or crew

Search for an actor, producer, director, or other member of crew, and you can see what films they've been in, created, or made a guest appearance.

### Add something to Up Next

While viewing a movie or TV show, tap the Up Next button in the top-right corner to add it to your Up Next list. You'll find this list on the Watch Now panel at the top of the screen.

# Maps, News, and Utilities

It doesn't seem so long ago that paper maps were the norm. Physical, cumbersome things which people carried around in their cars or backpacks. Now, with the iPad Pro at your fingertips, it's possible to navigate the globe and never get lost.

The iPad also makes for a powerful utility tool too. It has a helpful notes app, can check the latest news, and much more...

# Use Maps to navigate the world

Discover new places, get route guidance, and more...

With a map of the entire globe in your iPad, it's no longer possible to get lost in a busy city or strange new land. That's exactly what the Maps app gives you, alongside directions, real-time traffic information, transit timetables, 3D views of major cities and more. All of this for free and accessible at any time.

To find the Map app, just unlock your iPad then tap on this icon:

## The basics of using Maps

**1** Tap on the **search field** to search for a place, address, or landmark.

**2** This blue dot represents your current location in the world.

**3** Tap the **Info** button to change the view, toggle traffic, or mark your location.

**4** This is the main map view. You can pan and zoom using your fingers.

**5** Notice the information bar on the side of the screen. This automatically displays your recent activity, so you might see how long it will take to get home, where your car is parked, or where an event in your calendar is happening. You'll also find any collections of places you've saved alongside recently viewed locations.

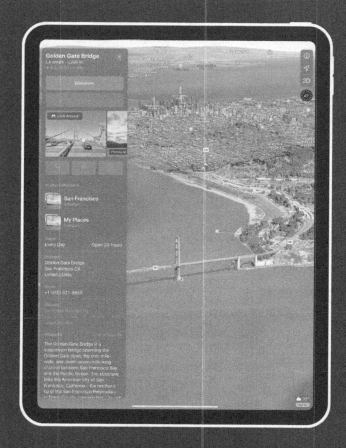

## See a 3D map

Using the Maps app it's possible to navigate the world's most famous cities in beautiful 3D graphics. To view the 3D map, ensure you're in satellite mode (see step above) then zoom in on the map. When you're close to the ground, you'll notice a **3D** button appear in the upper-right corner. Tap it and the Maps view will tilt, then load a 3D landscape with detailed 3D buildings. To rotate the image, simply place two fingers on the screen then rotate them. To tilt the camera, simultaneously move two fingers up or down the screen. Moving them left or right will pan the camera.

## Take a Look Around in first-person

Chances are you've seen Google's Street View. It's a great piece of technology that lets you explore the world at street level using full 360-degree imagery. Apple's Look Around mode is similar, but it's more polished, realistic, and includes tags for exploring businesses and interesting locations.

To use the Look Around mode, zoom the map until you see a binocular icon appear in the top-right corner. At the time of writing, it will only appear in major cities within the United States. Once you see it, tap the icon, and the map view will zoom down to street level.

To pan the view, just push it with your finger. To move in any direction, double-tap where you want to go. You can also tap on a tag to see more information about the place or business.

One last tip: tap the **minimize** icon in the top-left corner to shrink the Look Around view and place it above the 2D map. You can now move the Look Around view by panning the map with your finger.

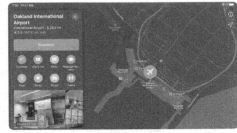

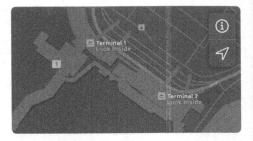

### Enjoy a flyover tour

Want to explore a city like never before? Simply search for the city's name then tap the **Flyover** button in the information panel at the bottom of the screen.

### Search indoor maps

With the Maps app you can find your way around airports and shopping centers using the indoor maps feature, which displays the locations of stores, toilets, and more.

### Look Inside

Most international airports and major shopping centers are fully mapped. Just look for a "look inside" badge that appears beneath the name of the location.

### Navigate floors

If there are multiple floors to the building, you can navigate through them by tapping the number button on the right-side of the screen, just beneath the info buttons.

### See Transit information

If you're exploring a location using public transport then it's a good idea to view the local area using the Transit view in Maps. This lets you see nearby train stations, tube lines, bus stations, taxi pick-up points and more. To enable this view simply tap the **Info** icon in the top-right corner of the screen then choose **Transport**.

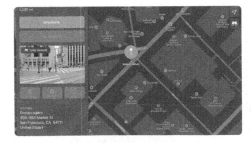

### Drop a pin to find out more

To see detailed information about a specific point, simply tap and hold your finger on the screen and a pin will be dropped underneath it.

### Share a location

Want to send an address to friends and family? Just search for the location then tap the **Share** icon in the information panel at the bottom of the screen.

### Search Maps using Siri

If you'd rather search for a place or person using Siri, hold down the **Power** button until Siri appears, then say something like "*where is the nearest hotel?*"

# Turn-by-turn navigation

Satellite navigation and GPS technology have made driving to unfamiliar locations so much easier; and with an iPad, you can take advantage of this same technology to explore and navigate the world. It's wonderfully easy to use. Once set up, Maps will display the route in 3D, with road signs and written directions. And if the traffic conditions change, Maps will offer an alternative route for you to take.

**1** To get started, open Maps then tap the **Search** field in the information panel. Next, enter the destination you wish the navigate too. This can be an address, zip code, or you can tap and hold on the map to drop a pin.

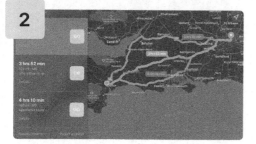

**2** Once you've searched for an address tap the blue **Directions** button to enable turn-by-turn instructions. Maps will automatically find the optimal route to the destination. It will also offer alternative routes, if any are available, which appear as opaque blue lines on the map. You can tap on these alternative routes to choose them.

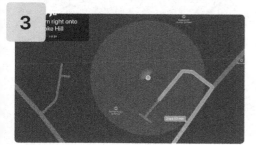

**3** Once you've found a suitable route tap the green **GO** button to begin following turn-by-turn directions.

Maps will automatically speak directions out-loud when you approach turns, lane changes, and exits - just as you'd expect if using a dedicated Sat-Nav device. You can even press the **Power** button to turn off your iPad display and it will light up whenever a change in direction is needed.

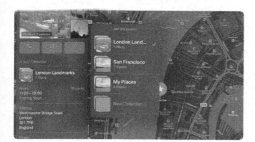

### Save a location as a collection

While viewing a location or pin, tap the **Add to** button, then either choose an existing collection or create a new one. You can view your collections at any time by pulling down the search field in the top-left corner.

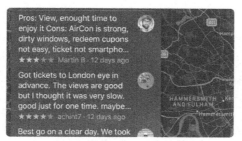

### Check out location reviews

If you're planning a trip to somewhere popular, search for it then pull the information panel upwards. Further down the panel you'll find a list of visitor reviews.

### Report an issue with the map

To report an error or missing place, tap the **Info** button in the top-right corner of the screen then tap **Report an Issue**.

# Get the latest News

## View the latest headlines and featured articles...

With the News app on iPad, you'll find all the latest news stories and featured articles in one place. That's because the News app automatically collects all the stories and topics you're interested in and presents them together. It also combines the rich design language typically found in traditional print, along with the interactivity of the web, to create an immersive experience where the story comes to life like never before.

To find the News app on your iPad, search for it using Spotlight, or look for this icon:

### Get started

Open the News app for the first time and you'll be greeted by the Get Started screen. From here you can add news sources, and sign up for an email newsletter than sends you the best stories each day.

### Add a news source

Once the app is set up and running it's just as easy to add and customize your news sources. Tap the **sidebar** button in the top-left corner of the screen, enter a channel or topic name then tap the plus icon.

### Remove news sources

To remove news sources tap the **sidebar** button, tap **Edit** at the top of the screen then tap the **delete** icon that appears alongside each channel or topic.

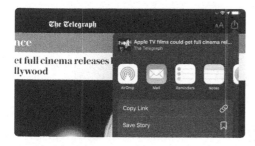

### Tell News what you like

If you really like a story or topic, tap the **share** icon at the top of the screen, scroll down then tap **Suggest More Like This.** Similarly, you can also tap **Suggest Less Like This** to hide similar stories.

### Save a story for later

Tap the **share** icon at the top of the screen, then tap **Save Story**. You can later find this story, along with any others you have saved, by tapping **Following**, then **Saved Stories**.

### Change the text size

If you're struggling to read the text within an article, tap the **AA** button in the top-right corner, then choose a larger font size.

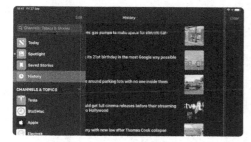

### See your reading history

If you read a story recently and want to re-read or reference it, tap the **sidebar** button, scroll down, then tap **History**.

### Tap and hold for extra options

Try tapping and holding on a story, channel or topic. You'll see a pop-up window appear with options for copying a link, following channels, opening a story in Safari and more.

### Check out Apple News+

With Apple News+ you can access more than 300 periodicals for $9.99 per month after a month-long trial. To find it just tap on the News+ button at the bottom of the screen.

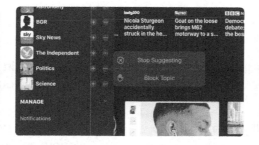

### See what channels Siri suggests

Siri will learn what topics and subjects you read over time, then recommend similar stories when you open the News app. You can see what Siri is currently suggesting by opening the sidebar then scrolling down to the bottom.

### Tell Siri to stop suggesting a topic

If you see a topic or channel in the Siri Suggestions panel that you don't like, tap on the **options** button, then tap **Stop Suggesting**.

### Manage your notifications

To specify which channels can send you notifications, open the sidebar, scroll down to the bottom, then tap **Notifications**.

# Monitor the Stock market

## Monitor the latest stocks and news, straight from your iPad...

Whether you're keeping an eye on the latest stocks, betting against them, or monitoring your portfolio, the Stocks app is a helpful way to track stocks and news.

The Stocks app comes pre-installed on every iPad. You can find it by looking for this icon:

Open the Stocks app, and the first thing you'll see is a sidebar listing the leading 13 stocks. To its right are the latest stock-related news stories.

To add a new stock, tap on the **Search** field near the top of the sidebar, and search for either the company name or its stock name. Once you've found it, tap the green **plus** button to add it.

## The basics of using Stocks

**1** If you need to check a stock, use this search bar to find it.

**2** Tap the **Edit** button above the search bar to organize your stock view.

**3** Here you'll find live updates of all your stocks. Tap on one to see more information.

**4** The News panel below the latest stock figures offers an overview of the latest stock news. Tap it to see more news, or tap on an article to read it straight away.

### See an individual stock

Tap on an individual stock and you'll see a graph of its latest performance. If it's colored green, then the stock is doing well. If it's red, then (you guessed it) it's not performing well.

### See an exact stock figure

Place your finger over a point on the share graph, and you'll see the exact figure of the stock during that day and time.

### See news stories related to stocks

Scroll down and you'll see news for that particular stock, tap on one and you can read the full story.

### Share a story

If you need to quickly share a stocks story with colleagues or contacts, open the story then tap the **Share** button in the top-right corner.

### Rearrange your stocks

To rearrange the Stocks on the home panel of the app, tap the small **menu** button in the bottom-right corner of the sidebar, then drag the stocks up or down using the sort buttons.

### Delete a stock

From the options panel you can also delete stocks by tapping the red **delete** buttons.

# Create your own Siri Shortcuts

Create complex actions then perform them using just your voice...

Think of Siri Shortcuts as an app that lets you create complex tasks and actions, then invoke them by asking Siri. So, you can do things like ask Siri "where's my next appointment" and the digital assistant will give you instant directions to the next event in your calendar. Similarly, you might say "turn today's photos into a collage", and Siri will automatically grab any photos from the day and turn them into a beautiful collage.

To find the Siri Shortcuts app, ask Siri to open it or look for this icon on the Home Screen:

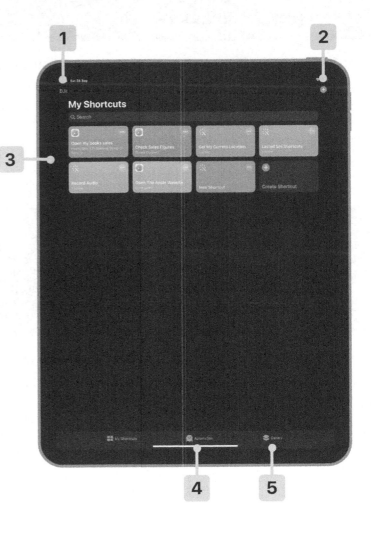

## The basics of using Shortcuts

**1** Tap **Edit** to delete or duplicate shortcuts.

**2** Tap the **plus** button to quickly create a brand new shortcut.

**3** Access your existing shortcuts here. You can also **tap and hold** on a shortcut to rename it, duplicate it, see more details or delete it.

**4** Tap the **Automation** button at the bottom of the screen to create an action that automatically runs at a certain time, place, event, or setting change.

**5** To discover a massive amount of Siri shortcuts tap the **Gallery** button then take a look around. You'll discover shortcuts based around accessibility, the home, daily routines and much more.

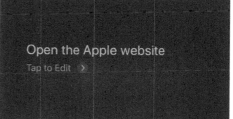

### Create a new shortcut

Let's create a new Siri shortcut that instantly opens Safari then goes to the Apple homepage. Start by tapping the **New Shortcut** button.

### Add an Action

In the New Shortcut screen, tap **Add Action**. You'll see a selection of suggested actions and shortcuts fill the screen. Tap the first one, called **Apps**.

### App actions

Look for **Safari** and tap it. Scroll through the list of Safari actions until you see **Open URLs**, then tap it.

### Enter an URL

Tap on the faint blue URL text, then enter "www.apple.com".

### Give the shortcut a Siri name

Tap **Next**, then type a name for you to call when you invoke Siri. In this example, let's call it "Open The Apple Website". Tap **Done** when you're finished.

### Invoke your new shortcut

You're now ready to test your new shortcut. Hold down the **power** button to access Siri, then say out loud "open the Apple website". With a bit of luck, Safari should instantly open and take you to Apple's site.

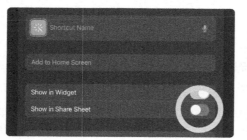

### Delete a shortcut

Just **tap and hold** on a shortcut then tap **Delete** in the pop-up window.

### Add a Shortcut to the Share Sheet

If you'd like to regularly invoke a Shortcut then adding it to the Share Sheet is a good idea. To do this **tap and hold** on a shortcut then tap the **Details** button. On the following screen toggle **Show in Share Sheet**.

### Here's another example...

Let's create a shortcut to share something via AirDrop. Create a new Shortcut, then select **Sharing > AirDrop**. Now, when you invoke this Shortcut while viewing something, the AirDrop panel will instantly appear on-screen.

# Create Reminders

Set yourself reminders so you'll never forget a thing...

The iPad already includes a notes app that can be used to jot down ideas and thoughts, but Reminders makes it easy to create to-do lists, set deadlines, and organize your life. It can also remind you with alerts at pre-determined times.

That's not all the app does, of course. It can group reminders into categories and even automatically sync reminders across all your devices via iCloud. To find the Reminders app, use Spotlight, or look for this icon:

## The basics of using Reminders

**1** Search for reminders, lists, or list items using the search bar at the top of the screen.

**2** Select a reminder or list here. You can also rearrange items by tapping, holding, then dragging.

**3** You can add additional items to a reminder list by tapping this **plus** button.

**4** To create a brand new reminder list, tap the **Add List** button in the bottom-left corner.

**5** You can rearrange or delete entire lists by tapping the **Edit** button.

**Create a new Reminder**

From the home screen of the Reminders app, tap the **Reminders** option under My Lists, then tap **New Reminder** in the bottom corner. Give it a name, then tap **Done**.

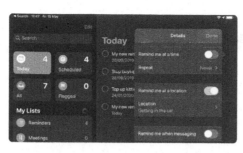

**Remind yourself at a date and time**

To remind yourself to do something at a specific date and time, tap on the new reminder, then tap the **i** button. On the next panel, tap **Remind me on a day**, then set a day and specific time if necessary.

**Remind yourself at a location**

Similarly, you can also remind yourself when you reach a location. To do this tap the **Remind me at a location** button, then either enter an address or choose from one of the suggested options.

**Share a reminder with someone**

Tap on the Reminder then tap the **options** button in the top-right corner. In the pop-up panel, you'll see an option to add people to the reminder. You can do this via email or third-party apps on your iPad.

**Create a subtask**

You can add a subtask to more complex reminders or lists. To do this tap on the reminder, tap the **i** button, then scroll down and choose **Subtasks**. Tap on it and then hit **Add Reminder** to add a subtask.

**Create a group of reminders**

From the home screen of the Reminders app, tap **Edit** in the top corner then hit **Add Group**. Give the group a name then tap **Create**. You can now drag and drop reminders into this group to categorize them.

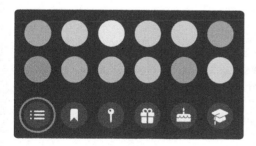

**Assign a color and icon**

From the home screen of the Reminders app, slide a reminder towards the left then tap the **info** button. In the pop-up window, you'll be able to re-name the reminder, assign a color and give it a unique icon.

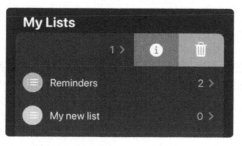

**Delete reminders**

From the home screen of the Reminders app, slide a reminder towards the left then tap the red **trash** icon to delete it. You can delete multiple lists and reminders by tapping **Edit** in the top-right corner.

**Create a reminder using Siri**

You can also add reminders by using Siri. Just hold the **Power** button, then say something like *"Remind me to pick up Sam"*. Siri will then automatically create a new reminder.

# Create, edit, and share Notes

## Learn how to quickly jot down notes, plus much more...

At first glance, the Notes app is a fairly basic way to jot down ideas and lists. It's much more than that, however. With the Notes app you can collaborate with friends, draw and annotate, scan documents, format text, create grids and more.

To find the Notes app, just look for this icon on the home screen of your iPad...

## The basics of using Notes

**1** You can open the Note sidebar by tapping this button.

**2** Collaborate and share a note with someone else by tapping this icon.

**3** Share, print, or save a note by tapping the **Share** button.

**4** Create a table within a note by tapping this icon.

**5** Format text with headings, style, or layouts by tapping the **Aa** button.

**6** Create a checklist of items by tapping the **tick** icon.

### Create a new note

To create a new Note, open the **Notes** app then tap the **New Note** button in the top-right corner.

### Sketch a note

If you'd like to draw into a note, tap **pencil** button on the top-right corner of the keyboard. A sketchpad will now appear on-screen, enabling you to draw with a pen, felt tip or pencil.

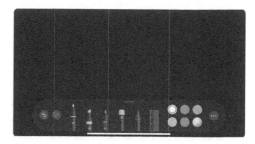

### Change the line color

You can change the color of the line by tapping one of the colored dots along the bottom of the screen. Tap on the multicolored circle to access additional colors.

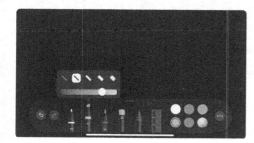

### Alter the brush thickness

Double-tap on a drawing tool and you'll be able to adjust its thickness and opacity.

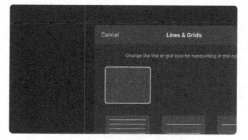

### See all your note attachments

To browse every sketch and photo attached to notes on your iPad, tap the **options** icon in the top-corner of a folder, then choose **View Attachments**.

### Insert a photo

To add a photo to a note just tap the **plus** icon, select **Photo Library,** then choose the relevant image.

## Create a table

It's surprisingly easy to create a simple table and embed it into a note. Start by creating or opening a note, tap where you want to insert the table then tap the **table** icon just above the keyboard. You'll then see a 2-by-2 table appear within the note.

You can add content to a row or column by tapping the appropriate area, or add additional rows and columns by tapping the buttons above or to the left of the table.

To copy, share, or delete a table, tap anywhere within the table itself, then tap the **table** icon above the keyboard. In the pop-up window simply choose the relevant option.

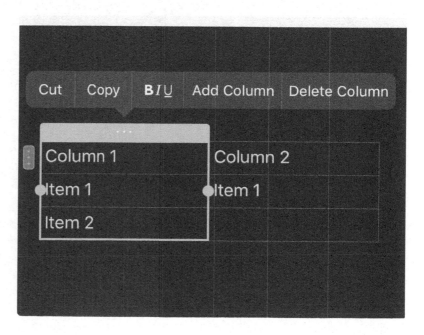

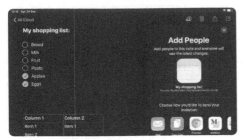

### Share a note

Want to send a note to someone else? Just tap the **Share** button and you'll see options for emailing the note, sending it to another device via AirDrop, or copying it.

### Print a note

While viewing a note, tap the **Share** button, scroll down then select **Print**. Please note that the iPad can only print to wireless printers connected to the same Wi-Fi network.

### Delete a note

While viewing the notes list just swipe across the note you wish to remove from right to left. Alternatively, you can tap the **trash** icon while editing a note.

## Collaborate on a note

If you'd like to share and collaborate on a note with friends and family then it's an easy process on iPad. If you're the creator of the note then it's yours to share, meaning you can invite others, see changes happen in real-time, and remove anyone at any time. Here's how it works:

**1** Select the note that you would like to share, then tap the **Collaborate** button at the top of the screen (it's next to the Trash icon).

**2** Use the Share panel to invite others from your Contacts book. You can also send invites via Message, Mail, Twitter and more.

**3** Anyone invited will receive an iCloud link to open your note. If they're using iOS then they can simply tap the link to open the note.

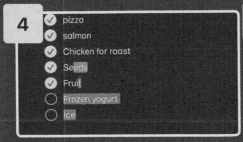

**4** As they make changes to the note you'll see them appear in real-time with a yellow highlight that fades away after a moment.

**5** To remove someone's permission, tap the **Collaborate** button, tap the person's name then choose **Remove Access**.

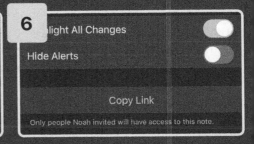

**6** If you're tired of seeing notifications everytime someone makes a change, tap **Collaborate** then un-toggle **Highlight All Changes**.

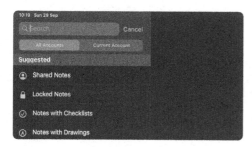

### Search for a note

To find a specific note, go to the home screen of a folder then pull down the notes list using your finger. You'll see a search field slide down from the top of the screen.

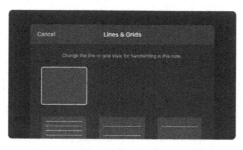

### Add a grid background to notes

You can add a variety of grid-based backgrounds to your notes. To do this tap the **share** button, scroll down, select **Lines & Grids**, then choose a style.

### Change the default Notes account

The default notes account is used whenever you create a new note. If for any reason you need to change it, go to **Settings > Notes**, then tap the **Default Account** option.

## Scan a document

Using the notes app, it's possible to scan letters and documents, then attach them directly to a note. What's great is that scans actually look like scanned documents, thanks to some clever post-processing which straightens the image and fixes any white balance issues. To scan a document:

While viewing a note, tap the **camera** icon above the keyboard.

Select the **Scan Documents** option.

When the camera view appears, move it over the document you wish to scan and your iPad will automatically recognize it.

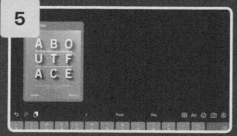

Tap **Keep Scan** to save the image. You can continue to scan further documents, or tap **Save** to attach the image/s to your notes.

The scan will now be attached to your note as an image.

# Manage your Files

Discover how to manage files stored on your iPad and in Cloud...

If you've ever used a desktop computer or laptop, then you'll feel at home using the Files app. It's basically a Finder app for the iPad, letting you organize, edit and delete files across all of your Apple devices and cloud services. You can find the Files app by searching for it using Spotlight, or by looking for this icon:

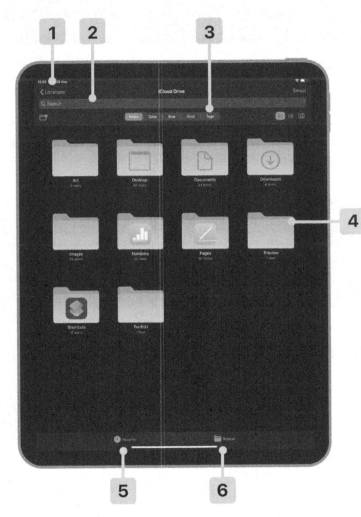

Open the Files app and you'll see the Browse screen, with shortcuts to search through your files, browse iCloud Drive, see local files on your iPad, and access any cloud-based services you have, such as Dropbox.

Files open or work in different ways depending on their file type. For example, images can be previewed, edited and marked up from within the Files app, while zip files can be previewed, but you can't extract their contents.

## The basics of using Files

**1** Quickly jump between files on your iPad, within iCloud, or browse your recently deleted files.

**2** Search for a file on your iPad or within iCloud using this search field.

**3** Browse and organize folders via name, date, size and tags. If you don't see these shortcuts, just pull the screen down.

**4** Copy, duplicate, rename, move, or delete a folder by tapping and holding on it.

**5** If you're in the Recents view, then you can get back to the **Browse** view by tapping this shortcut.

**6** See any recent files you've saved or modified by tapping the **Recents** shortcut.

### Swap to List or Column view

If you want to fit more things onto the screen, tap the **List** or **Column** view button in the upper-right corner of the screen. If you don't see it, pull the screen down with your finger.

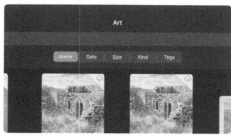

### Sort by size, date and name

While viewing a folder, you can use the tabbed buttons near the upper-center of the screen to sort your files by name, date, size, or tag color.

### Tap and hold for more options

You can **tap and hold** on both folders and files to copy/duplicate/delete them, see more info, add a tag, favorite them and even compress/uncompress them.

### See file information

If you want to see information about a file, such as its modified date or size and file type, **tap and hold** on the file until it lifts off the screen, let go then tap **Info** in the pop-up window.

### Create a folder

Creating a new folder to organize your files is easy, just pull the window down, then tap the **New Folder** button in the upper-left corner.

### Move a file into a folder

Tap the **Select** button at the top of the screen, select the file/s that you want to move, then tap the **folder** icon at the bottom of the screen.

## Drag and drop

One of the best features of the Files app is the ability to drag and drop files and folders. It makes organizing your files a breeze, lets you move multiple files at once, and tag files using a swipe. To get started, **tap and hold** on a file until it attaches to your finger. You can drag this file to another location, into a folder, or slide it over a colored tag.

You can also drag multiple files at once using Multi-Touch. To do this, **tap and hold on the first file**, then use one of your other fingers to tap on another file. You'll see it attach to the stack under your finger. You can keep doing this to add as many files as you like, then drag them to where they need to be and let go.

# Settings

Open the Settings app, and you'll find a wealth of options for customizing your iPad. It's possible to configure Notification Center, add security features, change screen settings, and much more.

The Settings app is also an important tool for customizing accessibility tools, enabling those with visual impairments to read small text or adjust the color output of the display to counter for color blindness.

# An overview of the Settings app

## Get to know the basics of Settings...

Whenever you want to make a change to your iPad, adjust a setting, or update the operating system, then the Settings app is the place to go.

You can easily find the Settings app by looking for the icon with a cog gear in the center:

Open the Settings app and you'll see a list of shortcuts to all the important settings on your iPad. They're labelled logically, so if you want to adjust how apps notify you, then tap on the Notifications shortcut. Similarly, if you want to connect to a new Wi-Fi network, tap Wi-Fi.

## The basics of using Settings

**1** Tap on your profile to access your Apple ID, where you can modify iCloud, iTunes, and device settings.

**2** Enable Airplane mode from here if you're boarding an aircraft, or need to save battery.

**3** Access Wi-Fi settings, connect to a new network, or remove existing Wi-Fi settings from here.

**4** Configure notifications from this shortcut. Other shortcuts from the Settings home screen include accessibility settings, Siri settings, and more.

**5** Drag the sidebar upwards to access additional settings, including individual app settings.

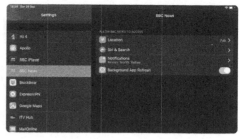

## Search through Settings

The Settings app is packed with toggle switches, fields, and features for customizing how your iPad works. Many are hidden away in sub-sections that you probably wouldn't find unless you were really determined, so if you need to quickly change a setting, open the **Settings** app and drag the screen down. A search bar will appear, enabling you to quickly find a setting or switch.

## Find individual app settings

To access individual app settings, open **Settings** then scroll down. Keep going and you'll find individual app settings. You can also search for an app by using the search box.

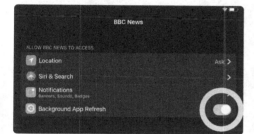

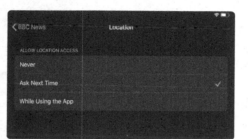

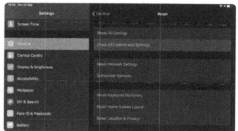

## Prevent apps from running in the background

If you're worried that an app is running in the background and using up battery, go to its Settings panel, then toggle **Background App Refresh** off.

## Prevent an app from tracking your location

From the same Settings panel, you can also prevent an app from tracking your location. You can choose to let an app track you all the time, when it's open, or never.

## Delete all of your data

If you're selling your iPad and want to wipe your data from it, go to **Settings > General > Reset**, then choose **Erase All Content and Settings**.

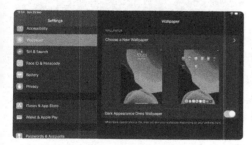

## Choose a new wallpaper

Changing the background wallpaper is always a great way to freshen the look and feel of your device. It's easy to do, just open the **Settings** app, tap **Wallpaper,** then **Choose a New Wallpaper**.

## Check for system updates

If you want to see if a new update is available for your iPad then go to **Settings > General > Software Update**. On the following panel you can download and install updates, or toggle Automatic Updates on.

## Update your Apple ID

Open the **Settings** app and tap on your **profile photo** to update and access all of your Apple ID settings. You can also manage your other devices and subscriptions from here.

# Use Screen Time to set limits

Discover how much time you've spent using your iPad, and limit distractions...

If you're concerned or worried that you might be spending too long using your iPad, then the Screen Time panel included in the Settings app will help you work out exactly how long you've spent using apps, how many notifications you've received, or set time limits to prevent future distractions.

## Find Screen Time

**1** Open the **Settings** app, then tap on **Screen Time**.

**2** Tap on your iPad at the top of the panel.

**3** You can then view your Screen Time data for the current day or the last 7 days.

As you'll see, the Screen Time panel is dense with information. You'll see total time spent with apps (some will be grouped into categories, such as "Productivity"), how many times you've picked up your iPad, and how many notifications you've received.

**Downtime**

Using the Screen Time settings panel it's possible to limit apps and notifications at a specific time, such as bedtime.

**Set a Downtime schedule**

Open the **Settings** app, tap on **Screen Time**, then choose **Downtime**. Toggle Downtime **on**, then use the Start and End buttons to set a schedule.

**Block inappropriate content**

If you would like to limit inappropriate content, such as R-rated films or adult websites, tap on **Content & Privacy**, toggle it on, then tap **Content Restrictions** on. On the following screen you'll find a massive number of restriction options.

# View an activity report of your iPad usage

Using the Screen Time panel it's possible to view daily or weekly reports of your iPad usage. You can see how long you've spent using apps, how many notifications you've received, and even how many times you've picked up your iPad.

**1**

Open the **Settings** app, then tap on **Screen Time.** At the top of the panel you should see a brief report on your iPad usage. Tap on **See All Activity** to see more details...

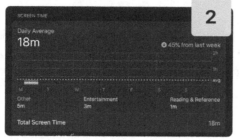

**2**

On the following panel you'll see a brief overview of the total time spent on your device, broken down into categories.

**3**

Beneath is a panel called Most Used. It displays which apps you've used the most during the day or last week. Tap on an app and you'll see a bar chart breakdown.

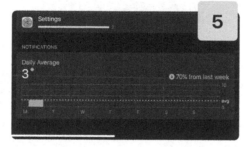

**4**

Below the Most Use panel is the Pickups panel. It displays exactly how many times you've pickcd up your iPad, as well as the average amount of time passed between each pickup.

**5**

Further below is report panel of the notifications you've received. It's broken down by app, so you can see exactly which app is sending you the most notifications.

## Other things you can restrict using Screen Time

By visiting the **Content & Privacy** panel in the Screen Time settings, you can limit or block a massive amount of content and features, including:

- App installation
- Location Sharing
- Changes to passcodes
- Account changes
- Mobile data limits

- Volume limit
- Explicit language
- Screen recording
- Multiplayer games
- Explicit entertainment and books

# See which apps are draining battery

Losing battery quickly? Here's how to see which apps are responsible...

The battery inside your iPad is massive, taking up most of its inside and being responsible for most of its weight. You'll typically get a days usage out of your iPad, but if you've noticed that the battery is draining quickly, then it's possible to see which apps are responsible. You can also work out how long you've spent using your iPad, and how long it has been asleep.

**Find the Battery panel**

Open the **Settings** app, then tap on **Battery**.

**Get a breakdown of app usage**

Scroll down slightly and you'll see a list of all the apps you've used, and how much battery they've used up.

**See how long an app was used**

Tap on the SHOW ACTIVITY button and you'll see how many minutes you've spent using each app.

## See your battery level over the last day

If you're worried that an app or service is using all your battery, then you can access a time chart which displays the battery level and activity over the last 24 hours, or 10 days. To do this:

**1** Open the **Settings** app, then tap on **Battery**.

**2** At the top of the screen you'll find two charts covering your batteries charge level and activity.

**3** You can toggle between the last 24 hours or 10 days using the tab buttonsabove the charts.

# How to use Do Not Disturb

Prevent or limit interruptions and calls...

It can be rather annoying when a message, FaceTime call or notification awakes you at night, or when your iPad Pro lights up and emits a noise during an important meeting. These notifications can usually be overridden by simply muting your device or putting it into Airplane mode, but the Do Not Disturb feature is simpler and much more effective.

It works by completely silencing your iPad between a determined period of time, for example, midnight and 7 AM. During this time, your iPad won't make a noise, light up or vibrate. Here's how it works:

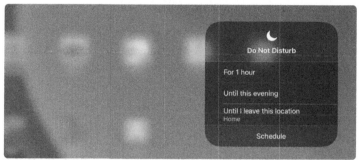

**Enable Do Not Disturb**

Swipe down to access Control Center, then tap the button which looks like a **crescent moon**. This will instantly enable Do Not Disturb, preventing any calls, messages or notifications from alerting you.

**Activate for just a period of time**

To quickly activate Do Not Disturb for the next hour, until the morning, or until you leave your current location, **tap and hold** on the **Do Not Disturb** icon in Control Center, then select an option.

### Exploring the Do Not Disturb panel...

To activate or schedule Do Not Disturb, go to **Settings** > **Do Not Disturb**, then toggle it **on**. You can then...

- **Schedule Do Not Disturb.** Use the **From** and **To** buttons to schedule Do Not Disturb, for example, when you go to bed.

- **Enable important contacts.** If you're expecting an important call, or need to let certain contacts get in touch at all hours, then tap the **Allow Calls From** button. On the next panel you can let anyone call, no one at all, or those in your Favorites list (created within the Contacts app).

- **Let repeat FaceTime calls through.** Contacts often call repeatedly when they urgently need to get in touch. You can let secondary calls through by toggling the **Repeated Calls** switch to **On**.

# Customize the Pointer

## Make it easier to see the pointer, or adjust its scrolling speed...

If you're using a Magic Mouse, Magic Keyboard or Trackpad to control your iPad, then it's possible adjust how quickly the pointer moves across the screen, its size, and even it's overall contrast.

### Adjust mouse scrolling speed

Open the **Settings** app, tap on **Accessibility**, then choose **Pointer Control**. Look for the **Scrolling Speed** slider, then adjust it to either increase or decrease the movement sensitivity.

### Adjust the pointer size

To make the pointer circle larger or smaller, go to **Settings > Accessibility > Pointer Control**, then adjust the Pointer Size slider.

### Increase the pointer contrast

If you're struggling to see the pointer as it moves across the screen, go to **Settings > Accessibility > Pointer Control**, then toggle **Increase Contrast** on.

### Change the pointer color

It's possible to swap the default grey pointer to either blue, white, red, green, yellow or orange accents. To do this, go to **Settings > Accessibility > Pointer Control**, then tap the **Color** option.

### Adjust the auto-hide timer

By default, the pointer will hide two seconds after it has moved. You can keep the pointer on-screen permantly, or adjust how long it takes to hide by going to **Settings > Accessibility > Pointer Control > Automatically Hide Pointer**.

### Disable pointer animations

With Pointer Animations enabled, the pointer morphs to match the shape of a hovered element, such as a button or app icon. If you'd rather it stay as a circular icon, go to **Settings > Accessibility > Pointer Control**, then toggle **Pointer Animations** off.

# Customize Trackpad Controls

Add additional features to your trackpad such as Tap to Click...

When you're using a trackpad with the iPad, such as a Magic Trackpad or the Magic Keyboard, a new panel is available in the Settings app. To find it open the Settings app and go to **General** > **Trackpad**. Here are some of the settings you can customize to ensure the trackpad works best for you...

**Turn off inertia animations**

By default, the pointer will slide to a halt, rather than stop abruptly, if you quickly lift your finger while scrolling. To disable this, go to **Settings** > **Accessibility** > **Pointer Control**, then toggle **Trackpad Inertia** off.

**Adjust trackpad scrolling speed**

If you'd like to adjust the speed of the pointer when using a trackpad, go to **Settings** > **General** > **Trackpad**, then look for the **Scrolling Speed** slider.

**Enable Tap to Click**

By enabling Tap to Click, it's possible to click on something by lightly tapping the trackpad with your finger. You'll find the Tap to Click option at **Settings** > **General** > **Trackpad**.

**Two-Finger Secondary Click**

The Two-Finger Secondary Click, you can initiate the long-press feature found throughout iPadOS.

### Find out more about a Mouse or Trackpad

Turn to page **64** to find out more about using a mouse or trackpad with your iPad.

# A guide to Accessibility settings

## Enable visual, audio, and physical accommodations...

Your iPad might be an intuitive device to use, but it's also packed with assistive features to help those with visual impairments or motor control limitations. You'll find the majority of them in the Accessibility panel within the Settings app. To get there, open **Settings**, tap **General**, then select **Accessibility**.

### Invert the colors of your screen

To flip the colors of your iPad's screen, go to **Settings > Accessibility > Display & Text Size**. You'll see two options: Smart Invert, and Classic Invert. Smart Invert will reverse the color of everything except images, media and a limited number of apps. Classic Invert will reverse the color of everything on the screen.

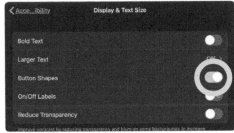

### Enable button shapes

Buttons in iOS usually look like a word or short piece of text. To make it more obvious which is a button and which is a piece of information, go to **Settings > Accessibility > Display & Text Size**, then toggle the **Button Shapes** switch **on**. This will display thin blue lines beneath buttons, and add small radio buttons to the inside of toggle switches.

### Bold text

A handy accessibility feature for those with vision impairments is the Bold Text toggle switch. Once activated, it makes text on the display appear to be bolder. To turn on Bold Text, go to **Settings > Accessibility > Display & Text Size**, then toggle **Bold Text on**.

### Show subtitles & closed captions

To enable subtitles and captions for entertainment on your iPad, go to **Settings > Accessibility > Subtitles & Captioning**, and toggle the top switch **on**.

### Style subtitles and captions

After enabling subtitles, tap the **Style** button to choose from three preset styles. By tapping **Create New Style** you can customize the font, size, color, and background style.

### Use slow keys to help you type

If it takes a while for you to type individual keys, then go to **Settings > Accessibility > Keyboards > Slow Keys**, and toggle it on. You can now adjust how long you have to press a key before it is activated.

## Adjust the color tint of the display to accommodate for color blindness

Color blindness can be a hassle at the best of times in the real world, and it's a problem that remains when using your iPad to browse the web, examine photographs or generally interact with the user interface.

Thankfully a built-in accessibility feature can adjust the color palette of the display to accommodate for color blindness, making it possible to see tricky colors in a wide range of spectrums. Here's how it works:

**1** Open the Settings app and go to **Accessibility > Display & Text Size > Color Filters** then toggle **Color Filters** on.

**2** You'll see a preview of the effect in the graphic at the top of the screen (scroll it left to see two color charts).

**3** To fine tune the color spectrum change, tap the filters below the image.

**4** You can adjust the intensity of the effect using the slider at the bottom of the screen.

## Connect a hearing aid to your iPad

By connecting a hearing aid to your iPad you can experience higher-quality FaceTime calls. Go to **Settings > Accessibility > Hearing Devices**, where you can connect to any Bluetooth-enabled hearing aids. Any hearing aids with HAC compatibility (visit support.apple.com/kb/HT4526 to see a list of compatible devices) will also enable you to increase and decrease the volume independently for both ears, monitor battery usage and more.

## Change the audio balance

If you're hard of hearing in one ear, or have a faulty pair of headphones, then it's possible to adjust the volume level in either the left or right channels. Go to **Settings > Accessibility > Audio/Visual**, then look for a slider with L on the left side, and R on the right. Drag it left or right to adjust the volume. It might help to play music via the Music app while you make the adjustment.

L                                                             R

## How to use Assistive Touch

Assistive Touch is a fantastic feature for those with impaired physical and motor skills. It enables you to activate Multi-Touch features such as pinch-to-zoom with only one finger. That's not all, it also enables you to trigger hardware features such as the volume buttons, and even rotate the screen or take a screenshot. It might sound complicated, but this feature is a doddle to use after a little practice.

To enable Assistive Touch, go to **Settings** > **Accessibility** > **Touch** > **Assistive Touch**, then toggle the button at the top of the screen.

You'll see a small square button appear on the side of the screen. By tapping this you can access a series of shortcut buttons which enable you to activate Notification Center, Control Center, Siri, functions on your iPad, return to the Home screen, or quickly access your favorite gestures.

## Create an Assistive Touch gesture

If you'd like to mimic a Multi-Touch gesture (such as zoom) using Assistive Touch, then it's possible to do this by using a custom gesture. To create one, go to the Assistive Touch panel in the Settings app, then tap the **Create New Gesture** button. On the following screen, use two fingers to mimic zooming out of an image. Once you've done, tap the **Save** button at the top of the screen. You can now use this gesture from the Assistive Touch panel by tapping the **Custom** button, indicated by a star.

## How to use Speak Selection

Siri is great for setting reminders, opening apps or finding out what's on at the cinema, but you can also use Siri to read out loud selected text, messages, and notes.

This feature, called Speak Selection, is particularly useful for those with impaired eyesight, but it's also a fun way to playback text and messages using Siri's voice.

To turn on Speak Selection go to **Settings** > **Accessibility** > **Spoken Content**, then toggle **Speak Selection**. To speak words out loud, highlight any text (by double-tapping or tapping and holding on it), then tap the **Speak** button in the pop-up menu.

You can also read Emojis out-loud to make friends and family laugh. To do this just double-tap on the **Emoji** to select it, then ask your iPad to speak the Emoji out-loud.

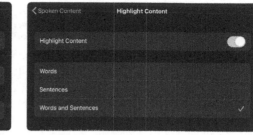

### Change the voice accent

Tap the **Voices** link and you can choose from a wide range of voices from the Speech menu. These include Australian accents, British accents, Spanish, Hindi and much more.

### Speak Screen

This helpful feature works by reading out-loud all the content that's currently on-screen. To enable Speak Screen, toggle its switch on from the **Speech** panel, then whenever you want to hear what's on-screen, swipe down from the top of the screen with two fingers. A panel will appear that enables you to control speech playback. To close the panel, simply tap the **X** button.

### Highlight words

Notice the **Highlight Content** button? Toggle this switch to see the words highlighted as your iPad reads them out-loud. Think of Karaoke and you'll get an idea of how this works.

## Use an on-screen magnifying glass

The iPad is designed to be easy for anyone to use, even those with visual impairments. However, there might be occasions where you need to zoom into the screen. Perhaps the text on a website is too small, or you can't quite make out the detail on an image. Those with visual impairments might also appreciate the ability to get a closer look at things on the screen. Using a three-fingered Multi-Touch gesture, it's possible to display an on-screen magnifying glass, which you can move around to examine things in more detail. Here's how to works:

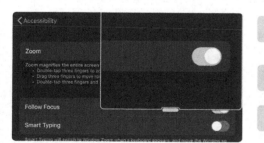

**1** Go to **Settings > Accessibility**, then tap the **Zoom** option near the top of the screen.

**2** You'll see a magnifying glass appear on-screen.

**3** You can move the magnifying glass around by dragging the small button at the bottom of it.

**4** You can hide the magnifying glass by tapping twice on the screen with three fingers.

# Notification Settings

## Change how your iPad and its apps notify you...

The iPad has become the centre of many people's digital lives, which means some of us are constantly bombarded with messages, tweets, updates, and notifications. These briefly appear as notifications at the top of the screen, but they're also available to see within Notification Centre, which is accessed by swiping down from the top-left corner of the screen.

If you'd like to modify how notifications arrive on your iPad, or turn them off completely, then open the **Settings** app and tap **Notifications**. Swipe the sidebar down to see a list of apps that display notifications. Select an app (such as Messages), where you'll see a large amount of notifications settings...

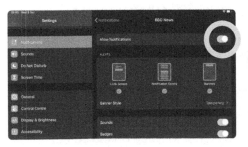

**Allow Notifications**

Perhaps it's obvious, but if you un-tick this button, the app will never send you another notification.

**Sounds**

If an app plays a sound effect when a notification arrives (for example a "ding!" when you get a text message), tap this shortcut to choose from a variety of sound effects.

**Badges**

This option enables you to turn off the red numbered badges which appear over app icons when you have a new notification.

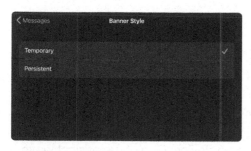

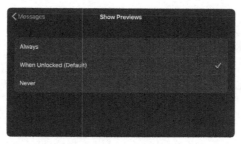

### Banner Style

Decide if notification banners appear for just a brief moment, or stay on the screen until you interact with them.

### Show Previews

If you don't want message content to appear in a notification, tap **Show Previews**, then choose **Never**.

### Repeat Alert

Your iPad will automatically alert you to new messages twice. You can disable or change this feature by tapping on **Repeat Alert,** then choosing another option.

## Modify Alert Style

This panel enables you to configure how notifications appear while you're using your iPad. You'll find three options:

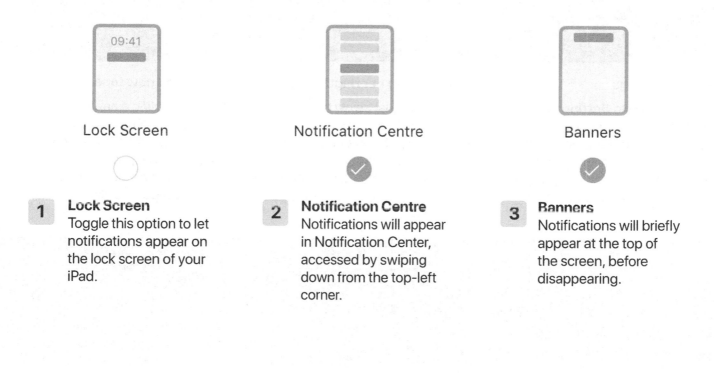

| Lock Screen | Notification Centre | Banners |
| --- | --- | --- |

**1 Lock Screen**
Toggle this option to let notifications appear on the lock screen of your iPad.

**2 Notification Centre**
Notifications will appear in Notification Center, accessed by swiping down from the top-left corner.

**3 Banners**
Notifications will briefly appear at the top of the screen, before disappearing.

# Audio Settings

## Personalize your iPad to sound a little different...

A little personalization can go a long way towards making your iPad feel like your own device. One of the easiest ways to do this is to alter the sound effects it emits. These include ringtones, email tones, tweet sound effects, calendar alerts, the lock sound, and keyboard clicks.

Over the next two pages, you'll learn how easy it is to select different tones and switch off sound effects that you might not need. You'll also discover how to set an automatic sound check feature, and set a volume limit.

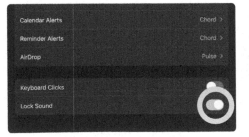

**Volume settings**

Begin by going to **Settings** > **Sounds**, where you'll see a large range of audio options appear on-screen. The slider near the top of the screen enables you to alter the volume level of all sound effects.

**Change a text or ringtone alert**

The buttons just below the volume slider enable you to choose from a wide variety of alert effects. Choose an option (such as **Text Tone**), then tap on a sound effect to preview and select it.

**Download new tones**

While selecting a new sound effect tone, tap the **Store** button to find new tones in the iTunes Store. Some are taken from popular music tracks, while others are custom sound effects purpose-built for your iPad.

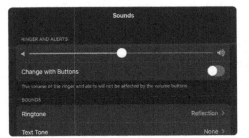

**Disable/enable Lock Sounds**

You can disable or enable the lock sound effect by toggling the **Lock Sounds** switch near the bottom of the screen.

**Turn off keyboard clicks**

Your iPad will automatically emit a keyboard click sound every time you press a key on the on-screen keyboard. You can disable this by toggling the **Keyboard Clicks** switch at the bottom of the screen.

**Change the music equalizer**

Go to **Settings** > **Music** > **EQ**. On the following panel you'll be able to choose from a number of equalizer settings. Not all are self-explanatory, so try playing an audio track in the Music app while choosing from the different options.

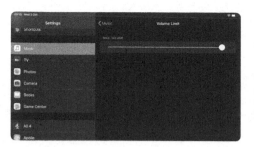

## Set a volume limit

Over time our hearing becomes less sensitive, but it can also be damaged by listening to loud music for long periods of time.

To prevent hearing damage while listening to music on your iPad, go to **Settings** > **Music**, then tap the **Volume Limit** button, then lower the setting by dragging the slider button to the left.

This will prevent your iPad from playing music at a volume higher than what is selected.

## Enable Sound Check

This clever feature will automatically scan your music files, then set an automatic level that lowers and increases the volume to make tracks and albums sound more coherent across the board.

From the **Music** panel in **Settings**, toggle the **Sound Check** switch to enable this clever feature.

# Troubleshooting

Most of us will never encounter a serious problem with our iPad. However, every now and then something might go wrong. Perhaps the battery doesn't last as long as it used too, or maybe a glass of water is spilled over the device. This brief chapter will cover the most common problems, and also explain how to book and attend a Genius Bar appointment.

# The Genius Bar

## Get help when you need it most...

The Genius Bar is a technical support service in every Apple Store where you can get help to solve a problem or receive a replacement device.

They're often referred to as the heart and soul of an Apple Store. Every Genius Bar is manned by a team of technical specialists called "Geniuses". Each has experience solving a wide variety of hardware and software-related problems. They're also friendly and understanding to boot.

Are the team at the Genius Bar actually geniuses? Ask, and you're likely to receive a shrug, a wink, or a bemused look; but these dedicated guys and gals solve even the most complicated problems on a day-to-day basis. If they can't fix a problem with your iPad then no one else can.

Most services at the Genius Bar are carried out for free. Repairs are carried out in the store, often while you wait. If the Genius can't repair the device on the spot, then a replacement is usually offered.

## Booking a Genius Bar appointment

The easiest way to book a Genius Bar appointment is via the Apple Store website. The URL changes depending on your location, but Google search "Book a Genius Bar appointment" and the first result should take you to the right page. From the website, you can select your nearest store and choose a suitable time and date – right down to the exact 10 minutes that suit your needs.

Please note that you'll need an Apple ID to book an appointment. This enables the Apple Genius to see your previous software and hardware purchases, which might prove to be helpful when diagnosing problems. It also makes paying for replacements and services much quicker.

Keep in mind that the Genius Bar is a popular service, so the first available appointment might be weeks in advance.

## Attending the Genius Bar

Before going to the Genius Bar, make sure to fully backup your device. You can backup your iPad via iCloud, or iTunes on a computer. Both methods save all your apps, text messages, photos, contacts, settings and more. These can be transferred to the new device once it's activated.

If you've never walked into an Apple Store then worry not. They're designed to be easy to understand and navigate. That is if the throngs of crowds aren't in your way. The front of the store is laid out with wooden tables with the most recent devices available to test and play with. Further back you'll see Macs and accessories, and on the back wall is the Genius Bar. If the store is configured in a different way (for example it has multiple rooms/halls), then look for the long wooden bench with black stools in front of it.

You check in with an employee holding a blue iPad. Can't see them through the crowd? Look for any other employee in a blue shirt, they'll be able to help. Alternatively, you can check in using the Apple Store app, but being met face-to-face is always more reassuring.

Once you're at the Genius Bar be polite and explain the problem with your device. The Genius team interview dozens of customers each day, sometimes hundreds. It's likely they've encountered every kind of problem, whether hardware or software related, and should be able to quickly identify what's wrong with a device. Research shows that a smile and positive attitude is the best way to get good customer service, and that applies to both employee and customer. Whereas creating a scene might get you thrown out of the store by security, a friendly chat could get you a free repair or additional advice.

# What happens to a water damaged iPad

## Try not to get it wet...

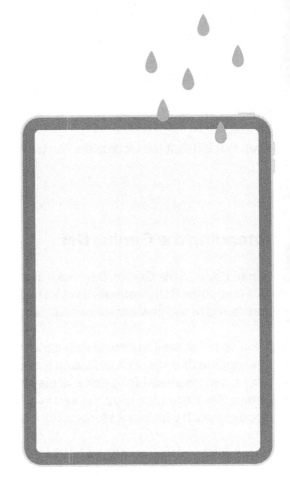

Water is usually a death sentence for electronic devices. That's because water conducts electricity, passing it instantly from one component to another causing them to overload. Impure water (such as fizzy drinks or sea water) also contains impurities that bind to electronics and corrode them. These impurities stay in the device even when it's dried, causing further damage over time.

Water damage typically causes the speakers and microphone to fail, can cause dark shadows to appear on the screen, or can break the device entirely. If you suspect this has happened, then it's a good idea to take your iPad to the nearest Apple Genius Bar for repair or replacement.

It's worth noting that every iPad and iPhone includes a liquid damage indicator. This is a small strip inside the Lightning Bolt port that changes color on contact with water. The Genius uses this strip to detect the presence of water when identifying problems with a device. So if you've dropped your iPad into very deep water there's little point pretending otherwise at the Genius Bar!

## Don't turn on a wet electronic device!

If you've accidentally dunked your iPad into liquid then you're probably okay to keep using as normal. Just blow it dry and hope for the best. If it has been in liquid overnight, then do the opposite! Don't blow into it or shake the device, because if water has leaked into the casing this will only move it around and potentially cause further problems.

## The best way to dry a wet iPad

First of all, avoid any heat sources. Hairdryers are hot enough to melt the solder inside an iPad. Similarly, avoid other heaters or sources of fire. Room temperature is your friend. The most efficient way to dry a wet device is to place it in a sealed container with silica gel packets. These are the same gels you find packaged with most large electrical devices. They typically come in small paper sachets.

If you don't have gel packets to hand, then white rice has been known to work. It's highly advisable to leave the device encased in rice for 24 hours, before repeating the process with a second portion of rice. Be patient, the longer you can leave the device to dry the more likely it will still work when it's turned back on. Good luck!

# Cracked Screen

## Try not to panic!

If you've never dropped an iPad then consider yourself lucky, for the sickening sound of glass and metal hitting a hard surface will make any stomach drop. It doesn't matter how strong a piece of glass is – it can, and will, break under certain conditions. Glass is particularly prone to knocks around edges and corners. On the iPad it's common to see breaks emanate outwards from the lock/mute button.

The iPad Pro uses Gorilla Glass for the construction of its screen. Gorilla Glass is created through a proprietary process that sees raw materials being blended into a glass composition that's microns thick. A chemical strengthening process then sees large ions being "stuffed" into the glass surface, before the glass is placed in a hot bath of molten salt at 400°. Needless to say, it's a complicated process that results in the strongest glass available in a consumer product. The process is refined and improved every few years, resulting in stronger versions of the glass that are subsequently manufactured into the latest devices.

Cracked screens are incredibly dangerous and should be fixed immediately. The fine cracks in Gorilla Glass will cut skin on contact, and it's possible that small pieces will fall out causing further problems. So, what's the best course of action when the glass screen on your iPad device is broken?

## AppleCare+

If you've already purchased AppleCare+ then congratulations, because a replacement screen for your device will cost you an excess fee of $29, plus applicable tax. If you've already broken the screen and wish to buy AppleCare+ then you're out of luck.

## Take your iPad to an Apple Store

The price of replacing a screen differs from one device to another. Older devices use separate components for the glass and LCD, whereas recent devices include composite screens that merge the LCD with the glass. This improves color reproduction and reduces glare, but increases repair costs. Here's a quick breakdown of the screen replacement costs for the iPad Pro:

- iPad Pro 9.7-inch: $379
- iPad Pro 10.5-inch: $449
- iPad Pro 11-inch: $499
- iPad Pro 12.9-inch: $599

# Other Problems

## How to quit troublesome apps, or even force your iPad to reboot...

It's rare, but sometimes hardware buttons stop responding or become stuck. Perhaps the Power button no longer clicks or the volume buttons stop working. If your iPad is less than a year old, or covered by AppleCare+, then a replacement is free. If older than a year expect to pay a replacement fee. Make an appointment with the Genius Bar to find out, or alternatively, try using the Assistive Touch accessibility feature (see Settings chapter for more information.) This enables you to trigger hardware buttons via touch-screen controls.

If your iPad has completely frozen and refuses to respond to taps or hardware buttons, then there are three solutions you can attempt:

### Force quit an app

If an app stops working, freezes or acts up, just swipe up from the bottom of the screen, then stop halfway to access the multitasking window. Next, slide the app which has crashed, up off the screen. This will force quit the app and remove it from the iPad's temporary memory.

### Reboot your iPad

Sometimes your iPad might stop responding to touch. This is very rare, but it does happen from time-to-time. In these extreme cases you can force the device to restart. To do this hold both the **Power** button and the **volume down** button simultaneously for between five and 10 seconds. When the iPad restarts you can let go.

### Let the battery run dry

If the hardware buttons are stuck or broken, then simply let the battery run dry. Note that this might take up to 10 hours.

# How to erase and restore an iPad Pro via recovery mode

When only the worst has happened...

This is a bit drastic, so only perform a wipe and restore if the Apple logo has been stuck on-screen for more than 10 minutes. Here's how it's done:

**1** Plug your iPad into a Mac or PC with iTunes running.

**2** Turn off your iPad if it isn't already (you might need to force restart it).

**3** Press and hold the **power** button for 3 seconds.

**4** While holding down the **power** button, press and hold the **volume down** button, for between 5 and 10 seconds.

**5** Let go of the power button but keep holding the **volume down** button for about 5 seconds (if you see the Plug into iTunes screen you've held it too long).

**6** If the screen stays black then you've done it - your iPad is now ready to restore using iTunes.

# Backup your iPad Pro to iTunes

In case you want a local copy of your iPad...

Your iPad will automatically back itself up to iCloud every time it's plugged in and connected to Wi-Fi, but nevertheless it's still a good idea to have a local backup on your Mac or PC in case of emergencies. Here's how to fully backup your iPad with iTunes on a desktop computer:

1. Plug iPad into your Mac or PC.

2. Launch **iTunes** if it doesn't automatically open.

3. If a message asks for your iPad's passcode, or to Trust This Computer, follow the on-screen steps.

4. Click on the **iPad** icon in the menu bar, then click on the **Summary** tab.

5. Look for the Backups box. Where it says Manually Backup and Restore, click **Back Up Now**.

## Restore your iPad from an iTunes backup

If you're having problems with your iPad then reverting to a local backup is a fairly straightforward process. Here's how it works:

1. Open iTunes on your Mac or PC then connect your iPad using its USB-C cable.

2. If a message asks for your iPad's passcode, or to Trust This Computer, follow the on-screen steps.

3. Click on the **iPad** icon in the menu bar, then look for the **Backups** field in the Summary tab.

4. Select **Restore Backup**, then choose the relevant backup if there are more than one saved.

5. Click **Restore**, then wait for the process to finish. You may be asked to enter the password for your backup if it's encrypted.

# What to do if you lose your iPad

First of all, don't panic!

It's probably somewhere obvious, like around the back of the sofa or in your backpack. If you've looked around and still can't find it then there are a few things you can try...

## Call it using FaceTime

**1** Open FaceTime on an iPhone, Mac, or another iPad.

**2** Tap the **plus** button, enter your own name or Apple ID, tap the blue link, then choose either **Audio** or **Video**.

**3** Listen for the call as it comes through to your iPad.

## Use Find My iPhone (for iPad)

Use another device or computer and go to www.icloud.com. Try to log in. If two-factor authentication is enabled and you're asked for a passcode, use your Mac or iPhone to get the code and enter it. If you don't have another iOS device or Mac, it's time to call Apple for further help.

Once you're logged into iCloud click the **Find iPhone** icon, then wait for your devices to load. Next, click on your **iPad** via the Map screen, or click the drop-down icon at the top of the screen and select it. In the pop-up panel, you'll be able to play a sound, erase your iPad, or place it into Lock Mode.

## Track your iPad in Lost Mode

If Lost Mode is enabled while your iPad is turned on and Location Services were activated then you'll be able to immediately track its location via the map screen. If Location Services were disabled when you turned on Lost Mode, then it's temporarily turned on to help you track the device. If your iPad was turned off completely, then Lost Mode will activate when it's next turned on and you'll be able to track it then.

## Erase your iPad

If the worst has happened and you don't think you'll be able to get your iPad back, then you can securely erase its contents to prevent someone from accessing your data. When erased an activation lock is enabled and Find My iPhone is automatically turned on. This means if your iPad is ever restored by someone else you can still track it and be assured that they can't unlock it without your Apple ID and password.

# Thanks for reading!

## That's it for now

So, you've come to the end of the book. Hopefully you've discovered a trick or two that will help you to really make the most of your iPad Pro.

If you would like to get in touch, have tips of your own, or have spotted a problem, please send an email via tom@leafpublishing.co.uk

**Published by:** Leaf Publishing LTD
www.leafpublishing.co.uk

**ISBN:** 9781549854774

**Author:** Tom Rudderham
**Editor:** Zeljko Jurancevic

**Copyright © 2020 by Leaf Publishing LTD**
All rights reserved. No part of this publication may be reproduced, stored or transmitted in any form or by any means, electronic, mechanical, photocopying, recording, scanning, or otherwise without written permission from the publisher. It is illegal to copy this book, post it to a website, or distribute it by any other means without permission.

**External Content**
Leaf Publishing LTD has no responsibility for the persistence or accuracy of URLs for external or third-party Internet Websites referred to in this publication and does not guarantee that any content on such Websites is, or will remain, accurate or appropriate.

**Designations**
Designations used by companies to distinguish their products are often claimed as trademarks. All brand names and product names used in this book and on its cover are trade names, service marks, trademarks and registered trademarks of their respective owners. The publishers and the book are not associated with any product or vendor mentioned in this book. None of the companies referenced within the book have endorsed the book.

**Humaaans Illustrations:**
Pablo Stanley
https://www.humaaans.com

# Index A-N

Quickly find what you're looking for...

# Index P-W

Quickly find what you're looking for...

Made in the USA
Coppell, TX
06 October 2020

39142855R00109